TWENTY-ONE DAYS IN INDIA

TWENTY-ONE DAYS IN INDIA,

OR THE

TOUR OF SIR ALI BABA, K.C.B.

BY

GEORGE ABERIGH-MACKAY.

GYAN

Published by

Gyan Publishing House
5, Ansari Road
Daryaganj, New Delhi-110002
Phone: 011-47034999, 9811692060
E-mail: books@gyanbooks.com

Distribution Network
gyanbooks.com
India, USA, Canada, UK, Australia

ISBN: 978-81-212-4924-9 (HB)
First Published, 1880

2nd Impression 2024

Printed at: Gyan Press, Delhi.

TWENTY-ONE DAYS IN INDIA
AUTHOR: GEORGE ABERIGH-MACKAY

TWENTY-ONE DAYS IN INDIA.

TWENTY-ONE DAYS IN INDIA,

OR THE

TOUR OF SIR ALI BABA, K.C.B.

BY

GEORGE ABERIGH-MACKAY.

THIRD EDITION.

REVISED AND CORRECTED BY THE AUTHOR.

LONDON:
W. H. ALLEN & CO., 13 WATERLOO PLACE,
PALL MALL. S.W.

1881.

PREFACE.

THE following papers were originally written, as will be gathered from the text, for *Vanity Fair*.

INDORE,
October 1880.

CONTENTS.

No. I.

THE VICEROY.

No. I.

THE VICEROY.

It is certainly a little intoxicating to spend a day with the Great Ornamental. You do not see much of him perhaps; but he is a Presence to be felt, something floating loosely about in wide pantaloons and flying skirts, diffusing as he passes the fragrance of smile and pleasantry and cigarette. The air around him is laden with honeyed murmurs; gracious whispers play about the twitching, bewitching corners of his delicious mouth. He calls everything by "soft names in many a musèd rhyme." Deficits, Public Works, and Cotton Duties are transmuted by the alchemy of his gaiety into sunshine and songs. An office-box on his writing-table an office-box is to him, and it is something more: it holds cigarettes. No one knows what sweet thoughts are his as Chloe flutters through the room, blushful and startled, or as a fresh beaker full of the warm South glows between his amorous eye and the sun.

> "I have never known
> Praise of love or wine
> That panted forth a flood of sweetness so divine."

I never tire of looking at a Viceroy. He is a being so heterogeneous from us! He is the centre of a world with which he has no affinity. He is a veiled prophet. He who is the axis of India, the centre round which the Empire rotates, is necessarily screened from all knowledge of India. He lisps no syllable of any Indian tongue; no race or caste, or mode of Indian life is known to him; all our delightful provinces of the sun that lie off the railway are to him an undiscovered country; Ghebers, Moslems, Hindoos blend together in one dark indistinguishable mass before his eye.

A Nawab, whom the Foreign Office once

farmed out to me, often used to ask what the use of a Viceroy was. I do not believe that he meant to be profane. The question would again and again recur to his mind, and find itself on his lips. I always replied with the counter question, "What is the use of India ?" He never would see—the Oriental mind does not see these things—that the chief end and object of India was the Viceroy; that, in fact, India was the plant and the Viceroy the flower.

I have often thought of writing a hymn on the Beauty of Viceroys; and have repeatedly attuned my mind to the subject; but my inability to express myself in figurative language, and my total ignorance of everything pertaining to metre, rhythm, and rhyme, make me rather hesitate to employ verse. Certainly, the subject is inviting, and I am surprised that no singer has arisen. How can anyone view the Viceroyal halo of scarlet domestics, with all the bravery of coronets, supporters, and shields in golden embroidery and lace, without emotion! How can the tons of gold and silver plate that once belonged to John Company, Bahadur, and that now repose on the groaning board of the Great Ornamental, amid a glory of Himalayan flowers, or blossoms from Eden's fields of asphodel, be reflected upon the eye's retina without producing positive thrills and vibrations of joy (that cannot be measured in terms of *ohm* or *farad*) shooting up and down the spinal cord and into the most hidden seats of pleasure! I certainly can never see the luxurious bloom of the silver sticks arranged in careless groups about the vast portals without a feeling approaching to awe and worship, and a tendency to fling small coin about with a fine mediæval profusion. I certainly can never drain those profound golden cauldrons seething with champagne without a tendency to break into loud expressions of the inward music and conviviality that simmer in my soul. Salutes of cannon, galloping escorts, processions of landaus, beautiful teams of English horses, trains of private saloon carriages (cooled with water trickling over sweet jungle grasses) streaming through the sunny land, expectant crowds of beauty with hungry eyes making a delirious welcome at every stage, the whole country blooming into dance and banquet and fresh girls at every step taken—these form the fair guerdon that stirs my breast at certain moments and makes me often resolve, after dinner, "to scorn delights and live laborious days," and sell my beautiful soul, illuminated with art and poetry, to the devil of Industry, with reversion to the supreme secretariat.

How mysterious and delicious are the cool penetralia of the Viceregal Office! It is the sensorium of the Empire; it is the seat of thought; it is the abode of moral responsibility! What battles, what famines, what excursions, of pleasure, what banquets and pageants, what concepts of change have sprung into life here! Every pigeon-hole contains a potential revolution; every office-box cradles the embryo of a war or dearth. What shocks and vibrations, what deadly thrills does this little thunder-cloud office transmit to far-away provinces lying beyond rising and setting suns. Ah! Vanity, these are pleasant lodgings for five years, let who may turn the kaleidoscope after us.

A little errant knight of the press who has just arrived on the Delectable Mountains, comes rushing in, looks over my shoulder, and says, "A deuced expensive thing a Viceroy." This little errant knight would take the thunder at a quarter of the price, and keep the Empire paralytic with change and fear of change as if the great Thirty-thousand-pounder himself were on Olympus.

No. II.

THE A.D.C.-IN-WAITING,

AN ARRANGEMENT IN SCARLET AND GOLD.

No. II.

THE A.D.C.-IN-WAITING.

AN ARRANGEMENT IN SCARLET AND GOLD.

THE tone of the A.D.C. is subdued. He stands in doorways and strokes his moustache. He nods sadly to you as you pass. He is preoccupied with—himself. He has a motherly whisper for Secretaries and Members of Council. His way with ladies is sisterly—undemonstratively affectionate. He tows up rajas to H.E., and stands in the offing. His attitude towards rajas is one of melancholy reserve. He will perform the prescribed observances, if he cannot approve of them. Indeed, generally, he disapproves of the Indian people, though he condones their existence. For a brother in aiguillettes there is a Masonic smile and a half-embarrassed familiarity, as if found out in acting his part. But confidence is soon restored with melancholy glances around, and profane persons who may be standing about move uneasily away.

An A.D.C. should have no tastes. He is merged in "the house." He must dance and ride admirably; he ought to shoot; he may sing and paint in water-colours, or botanise a little, and the faintest aroma of the most volatile literature will do him no harm; but he cannot be allowed preferences. If he has a weakness for very pronounced collars and shirt-cuffs in mufti, it may be connived at, provided he be honestly nothing else but the man in collars and cuffs.

When a loud, joyful, and steeplechasing Lord, in the pursuit of pleasure and distant wars, dons the golden cords for a season, the world understands that this is masquerading, skittles, and a joke. One must not confound the ideal A.D.C. with such a figure.

The A.D.C. has four distinct aspects or

phases—(1) the full summer sunshine and bloom of scarlet and gold for Queen's birthdays and high ceremonials; (2) the dark frock-coat and belts in which to canter behind his Lord; (3) the evening tail-coat, turned down with light blue and adorned with the Imperial arms on gold buttons; (4) and, finally, the quiet disguises of private life.

It is in the sunshine glare of scarlet and gold that the A.D.C. is most awful and unapproachable; it is in this aspect that the splendour of vice-imperialism seems to beat upon him most fiercely. The Rajas of Rajputana, the diamonds of Golconda, the gold of the Wynaad, the opium of Malwa, the cotton of the Berars, and the Stars of India seem to be typified in the richness of his attire and the conscious superiority of his demeanour. Is he not one of the four satellites of that Jupiter who swims in the highest azure fields of the eastern heavens?

Frock-coated and belted, he passes into church or elsewhere behind his Lord, like an aërolite from some distant universe, trailing cloudy visions of that young lady's Paradise of bright lights and music, champagne, mayonnaise, and "just-one-more-turn," which is situated behind the flagstaff on the hill.

The tail-coat, with gold buttons, velvet cuffs, and light-blue silk lining, is quite a demi-official, small-and-early arrangement. It is compatible with a patronising and somewhat superb flirtation in the verandah; nay, even under the pine-trees beyond the *Gurkha* sentinel, whence many-twinkling Jakko may be admired; it is compatible with a certain shadow of human sympathy and weakness. An A.D.C. in tail-coat and gold buttons is no longer a star; he is only a fire-balloon; though he may twinkle in heaven, he can descend to earth. But in the quiet disguises of private life he is the mere stick of a rocket. He is quite of the earth. This scheme of clothing is compatible with the tenderest offices of gaming or love—offices of which there shall be no recollection on the re-assumption of uniform and on re-apotheosis. An A.D.C. in plain clothes has been known to lay the long odds at whist, and to qualify, very nearly, for a co-respondentship.

In addition to furnishing rooms in his own person, an A.D.C. is sometimes required to copy my Lord's letters on mail-day, and, in due subordination to the Military Secretary, to superintend the stables, kitchen, or Invitation Department.

After performing these high functions, it is hard if an A.D.C. should ever have to revert to the buffooneries of the parade-ground, or to the vulgar intimacies of a mess. It is hard that one who has for five years been identified with the Empire should ever again come to be regarded as "Jones of the 10th," and spoken of as "Punch" or "Bobby" by old boon companions. How can a man who has been behind the curtain, and who has seen *la première danseuse* of the Empire practising her steps before the manager Strachey, in familiar chaff and talk with the Council ballet, while the little scene-painter and Press Commissioner stood aside with cocked ears, and the privileged violoncellist made his careless jests—how, I say, can one who has thus been above the clouds on Olympus ever associate with the gaping, chattering, irresponsible herd below?

It is well that our Ganymede should pass away from heaven into temporary eclipse; it is well that before being exposed to the rude gaze of the world he should moult his rainbow plumage in the Cimmeria of the Rajas. Here we shall see him again, a blinking *ignis fatuus* in a dark land—"so shines a good deed in a naughty world," thinks the Foreign Office.

No. III.

THE COMMANDER-IN-CHIEF.

No. III.

THE COMMANDER-IN-CHIEF.

At Simla and Calcutta the Government of India always sleeps with a revolver under its pillow—that revolver is the Commander-in-Chief. There is a tacit understanding that this revolver is not to be let off; indeed, sometimes it is believed that this revolver is not loaded.

The Commander-in-Chief is himself an army. His transport, medical attendance, and provisioning are cared for departmentally, and watched over by responsible officers. He is a host in himself; and a corps of observation.

All the world observes him. His slightest movement creates a molecular disturbance in type, and vibrates into newspaper paragraphs.

When Commanders-in Chief are born the world is unconscious of any change. No one knows when a Commander-in-Chief is born. No joyful father, no pale mother has ever experienced such an event as the birth of a Commander-in-Chief in the family. No Mrs Gamp has ever leant over the banister and declared to the expectant father below that it was "a fine healthy Commander-in-Chief." Therefore, a Commander-in-Chief is not like a poet. But when a Commander-in-Chief dies, the spirit of a thousand Beethovens sobs and wails in the air; dull cannon roar slowly out their heavy grief; silly rifles gibber and chatter demoniacally over his grave; and a cocked hat, emptier than ever, rides with the mockery of despair on his coffin.

On Sunday evening, after tea and catechism, the Supreme Council generally meet for riddles and forfeits in the snug little cloak-room parlour at Peterhoff. "Can an army tailor make a Commander-in-Chief?" was once asked. Eight old heads were scratched and searched, but no answer was found. No sound was heard save the seething whisper of champagne ebbing and flowing in the eight old heads. Outside, the wind moaned through the rhododendron trees; within, the Commander-in-Chief wept peacefully. He felt the awkwardness of the situation. An aide-de-camp stood at the door hiccupping idly. He was known to have invested all his paper currency in Sackville Street; and he felt in honour bound to say that the riddle was a little hard on the army tailors. So the subject dropped.

A Commander-in-Chief is one of the most beautiful articles of social upholstery in India. He sits in a large chair in the drawing-room. Heads and bodies sway vertically in passing him. He takes the oldest woman in to dinner; he gratifies her with his drowsy cackle. He says "Yes" and "No" to everyone with drowsy civility; everyone is conciliated. His stars dimly twinkle—twinkle; the host and hostess enjoy their light. After dinner he decants claret into his venerable person, and tells an old story; the company smile with innocent joy. He rejoins the ladies and leers kindly on a pretty woman; she forgives herself a month of indiscretions. He touches Lieutenant the Hon. Jupiter Smith on the elbow and inquires after his mother; a noble family is gladdened. He is thus a source of harmless happiness to himself and to those around him.

If a round of ball cartridge has been wasted by a suicide, or a pair of ammunition boots carried off by a deserter, the Commander-in-Chief sometimes visits a great cantonment under a salute of seventeen guns. The military then express their joy in their peculiar fashion, according to their station in life. The cavalry soldier takes out his charger and gallops heedlessly up and down all the roads in the station. The sergeants of all arms fume about as if transacting some important business between the barracks and their officers' quarters. Subalterns hang about the Mess, whacking their legs with small pieces of cane and drinking pegs with mournful earnestness. The Colonel sends for everyone who has not the privilege of sending for him; and says nothing to each one, sternly and decisively. The Majors, and the officers doing general duty, go to the Club and swear before the civilians that they are worked off their legs, complaining fiercely to themselves that the Service is going, &c. &c. The Deputy-Assistant-Quartermaster-General puts on all the gold lace he is allowed to wear, and gallops to the Assistant-Adjutant-General,—where he has tiffin. The Major-General-Commanding writes notes to each of his friends, and keeps orderlies flying at random in every direction.

The Commander-in-Chief—who had a disturbed night in the train—sleeps peacefully throughout the day, and leaves under another salute in the afternoon. He shakes hands with everyone he can see at the station, and jumps into a long saloon carriage, followed by his staff.

"A deuced active old fellow!" everyone says; and they go home and dine solemnly with one another under circumstances of extraordinary importance.

The effect of the Commander-in-Chief is very remarkable on the poor Indian, whose untutored mind sees a Lord in everything. He calls the Commander-in-Chief "the Jungy Lord," or War-Lord, in contradistinction to the "Mulky-Lord," or Country-Lord, the appellation of the Viceroy. To the poor Indian this War-Lord is an object of profound interest and speculation. He has many aspects that resemble the other and more intelligible Lord. An aide-de-camp rides behind him; hats, or hands, rise electrically as he passes; yet it is felt in secret that he is not pregnant with such thunder-clouds of rupees, and that he cannot make or mar a Raja. To the Raja it is an ever-recurring question whether it is necessary or expedient to salaam to the Jungy Lord and call upon him. He is hedged about with servants who will require to be richly propitiated before any dusky countryman gets access to this Lord of theirs. Is it, then, worth while to pass through this fire to the possible Moloch who sits beyond? Will this process of parting with coin—this Valley of the Shadow of Death—lead them to any palpable advantage? Perhaps the War-Lord with his red right hand can add guns to their salute; perhaps he will speak a recommendatory word to his caste-fellow, the Country Lord? These are precious possibilities.

A Raja whom I am now prospecting for the Foreign Office asked me the other day where Commanders-in-Chief were ripened, seeing that they were always so mellow and blooming. I mentioned a few nursery gardens I knew of in and about Whitehall and Pall Mall. H.H. at once said that he should like to plant his son there, if I would water him with introductions. This is young 'Arry Bobbery, already favourably known on the Indian Turf as an enterprising and successful defaulter.

You will know 'Arry Bobbery if you meet him, dear Vanity, by the peculiarly gracious way in which he forgives and forgets should you commit the indiscretion of lending him money. You may be sure that he will never allude to the matter again, but will rather wear a piquant do-it-again manner, like our irresistible little friend Conny B——. I don't believe, however, that Bobbery will ever become a Commander-in-Chief, though his distant cousin, Scindia, is a General, and though they talk of pawning the 'long-shore Governorship of Bombay to Sir Cursingjee Damtheboy.

No. IV.

THE ARCHDEACON,

A MAN OF BOTH WORLDS.

No. IV.

THE ARCHDEACON,

A MAN OF BOTH WORLDS.

THE Press Commissioner has been trying by a strained exercise of his prerogative to make me spend this day with the Bishop, and not with the Archdeacon; but I disregard the Press Commissioner; I make light of him; I treat his authority as a joke. What authority has a pump? Is a pump an analyst and a coroner?

Why should I spend a day with the Bishop? What claim has the Bishop on my improving conversation? I am not his sponsor. Besides, he might do me harm—I am not quite sure of his claret. I admit his superior ecclesiastical birth; I recollect his connection with St. Peter; and I am conscious of the more potent spells and effluences of his shovel-hat and apron; but I find the atmosphere of his heights cold, and the rarefied air he breathes does not feed my lungs. Up yonder, above the clouds of human weakness, my vertebræ become unhinged, my bones inarticulate, and I collapse. I meet missionaries, and I hear the music of the spheres; and I long to descend again to the circles of the every-day inferno where my friends are.

> "These distant stars I can forego;
> This kind, warm earth is all I know."

I am sorry for it. I really have upward tendencies; but I have never been able to fix upon a balloon. The High Church balloon always seems to me too light; and the Low Church balloon too heavy; while no experienced aëronaut can tell me where the Broad Church balloon is bound for; thus, though a featherweight sinner, here I am upon the firm earth.

So come along, my dear Archdeacon, let us have a stroll down the Mall, and a chat about Temporalities, Fabrics, "Mean Whites," and little Mrs. Lollipop, "the joy of wild asses."

An Archdeacon is one of the busiest men in India—especially when he is up on the hill among the sweet pine-trees. He is the recognised guardian of public morality; and the hill captains and the semi-detached wives lead him a rare life. There is no junketing at Goldstein's, no picnic at the waterfalls, no games at Ammandale, no rehearsals at Herr Felix von Batten's, no choir practice at the church even, from which he can safely absent himself. A word, a kiss, some matrimonial charm dispelled—these electric disturbances of society must be averted. The Archdeacon is the lightning conductor; where he is, the levin of naughtiness passes to the ground, and society is not shocked.

In the Bishop and the ordinary padré we have far-away people of another world. They know little of us; we know nothing of them. We feel much constraint in their presence. The presence of the ecclesiastical sex imposes severe restrictions upon our conversation. The Lieutenant-Governor of the South-Eastern Provinces once complained to me that the presence of a clergyman rendered nine-tenths of his vocabulary contraband, and choked up his fountains of anecdote. But with an Archdeacon all this is changed. He is both of Heaven and Earth. When we see him in the pulpit we are pleased to think that we are with the angels; when we meet him in a ball-room we are flattered to feel that the angels are with us. When he is with us—though, of course, he is not of us—he is yet exceedingly like us. He may seem a little more venerable than he is; perhaps there may be about him a grandfatherly air that his years do not warrant; he may exact a "Sir" from us that is not given to others of his worldly standing; but there is nevertheless that in his bright and kindly eye—there is that in his side-long glance—which by a charm of Nature transmutes homage into familiar friendship, and respect into affection.

The character of Archdeacons, as clergymen, I would not venture to touch upon. It is proverbial that Archidiaconal functions are

Eleusinian in their mysteriousness. No one, except an Archdeacon, pretends to know what the duties of an Archdeacon are; so no one can say whether these duties are performed perfunctorily and inadequately, or scrupulously and successfully. We know that Archdeacons sometimes preach, and that is about all we know. I know an Archdeacon in India who can preach a good sermon—I have heard him preach it many a time, once on a benefit night for the Additional Clergy Society. It wrung four annas from me—but it was a terrible wrench. I would not go through it again to have every living graduate of St. Bees and Durham disgorged on our coral strand.

From my saying this do not suppose that I am Mr. Whitley Stokes, or Babu Keshab Chandra Sen. I am a Churchman, beneath the surface, though a pellicle of inquiry may have supervened. I am not with the party of the Bishop, nor yet am I with Sir J. S., or Sir A. C. I abide in the Limbo of Vanity, as a temporary arrangement, to study the seamy side of Indian politics and morality, to examine misbegotten wars and reforms with the scalpel, Stars of India with the spectroscope, and to enjoy the society of half-a-dozen amusing people to whom the Empire of India is but as a wheel of fortune.

I like the recognised relations between the Archdeacon and women. They are more than avuncular and less than cousinly; they are tender without being romantic, and confiding without being burdensome. He has the private *entrée* at *chhoti hazri*, or early breakfast; he sees loose and flowing robes that are only for esoteric disciples; he has the private *entrée* at five o'clock tea, and hears plans for the evening campaign openly discussed. He is quite behind the scenes. He hears the earliest whispers of engagements and flirtations. He can give a stone to the Press Commissioner in the gossip handicap, and win in a canter. You cannot tell him anything he does not know already.

Whenever the Government of India has a merrymaking, he is out on the trail. At Delhi he was in the thick of the mummery, beaming on barbaric princes and paynim princesses, blessing banners, blessing trumpeters, blessing proclamations, blessing champagne and truffles, blessing pretty girls, and blessing the conjunction of planets that had placed his lines in such pleasant places. His tight little cob, his perfect riding kit, his flowing beard, and his pleasant smile were the admiration of all the Begums and Nabobs that had come to the fair. The Government of India took such delight in him that they gave him a gold medal and a book.

With the inferior clergy the Archdeacon is not at his ease. He cannot respect the little ginger-bread gods of doctrine they make for themselves; he cannot worship at their hill altars; their hocus-pocus and their crystallised phraseology fall dissonantly on his ear; their talk of chasubles and stoles, eastern attitude, and all the rest of it, is to him as a tale told by an idiot, full of sound and fury, signifying nothing. He would like to see the clergy merely scholars and men of sense set apart for the conduct of divine worship and the encouragement of all good and kindly offices to their neighbours; he does not wish to see them mediums and conjurers. He thinks that in a heathen country their paltry fetishism and incomprehensible technicalities are peculiarly offensive and injurious to the interests of civilisation and Christianity. Of course the Archdeacon may be very much mistaken in all this; and it is this generous consciousness of fallibility which gives the singular charm to his religious attitude. He can take off his ecclesiastical spectacles and perceive that he may be in the wrong like other men.

Let us take a last look at the Archdeacon, for in the whole range of prominent Anglo-Indian characters our eye will not rest upon a more orbicular and satisfactory figure.

> "A good Archdeacon, nobly planned
> To warn, to comfort, and command;
> And yet a spirit gay and bright,
> With something of the *candle*-light.'

No. V.

THE SECRETARY TO GOVERNMENT.

No. V.

THE SECRETARY TO GOVERNMENT.

He is clever, I am told; and being clever he has to be rather morose in manner and careless in dress, or people might forget that he was clever. He has always been clever. He was the clever man of his year. He was so clever when he first came out that he could never learn to ride, or speak the Indian language, and had to be translated to the Provincial Secretariat. But though he could never speak an intelligible sentence in the vernacular, he had such a practical and useful knowledge of it, in half-a-dozen of its dialects, that he could pass examinations in it with the highest credit, netting immense rewards. He thus became not only more and more clever, but more and more solvent; until he was an object of wonder to his contemporaries, of admiration to the Lieutenant-Governor, and of desire to several *Barri Mem Sahibs* with daughters. It was about this time that he is supposed to have written an article published in some English periodical. It was said to be an article of a solemn description; and report magnified the periodical into the *Quarterly Review*. So he became one who wrote for the English Press. It was felt that he was a man of letters; it was assumed that he was on terms of familiar correspondence with all the chief literary men of the day. With so conspicuous a reputation, he believed it necessary to do something in religion. So he gave up religion, and allowed it to be understood that he was a man of advanced views; a Positivist, a Buddhist, or something equally occult. Thus he became ripe for the highest employment, and was placed successively on a number of Special Commissions. He inquired into everything; he wrote hundredweights of reports; he proved himself to have the true paralytic ink flux, precisely the kind of wordy discharge, or brain hæmorrhage, required of a high official in India. He would write ten pages where a clod-hopping collector would write a sentence. He could say the same thing over and over again in a hundred different ways. The feeble forms of official satire were at his command. He desired exceedingly to be thought supercilious, and he thus became almost necessary to the Government of India, was canonised, and caught up to Simla. The Indian papers chanted little anthems, "the Services" said "Amen," and the apotheosis was felt to be a success. On reaching Simla he was found to be familiar with the two local "jokes," planted many years ago by some jackass. One of these "jokes" is about everything in India having its peculiar smell, except a flower; the second is some inanity about the Indian Government being a despotism of despatch-boxes tempered by the loss of the keys. He often emitted these mournful "jokes" until he was declared to be an acquisition to Simla society.

Such is the man I am with to-day. His house is beautifully situated, overlooking a deep ravine, full of noble pine-trees; and it is surrounded by rhododendrons. The verandah is gay with geraniums and tall servants in Imperial red deeply encrusted with gold. Within, all is very respectable and nice, only the man is—not exactly vile, but certainly imperfect in a somewhat conspicuous degree. With the more attractive forms of sin he has no true sympathy. I can strike no concord with him on this umbrageous side of nature. I am seriously shocked to discover this, for he affects infirmity; but his humanity is weak. In his character I perceive the perfect animal outline, but the colour is wanting; the glorious sunshine, the profound glooms of humanity are not there.

Such a man is dangerous; he decoys you into confidences. Even Satan cannot respect a sinner of this complexion,—a sinner who is only fascinated by the sinfulness of sin. As for my poor host, I can see that he has never really graduated in sin at all; he has only sought the degree of sinner *honoris causa.* I am sure that he never had enough true vitality or enterprise to sin as a man ought to sin, if he does sin. When I speak of sin I will be understood to mean the venial offences of prevarication and sleeping in church. I am not thinking of sheep-stealing or highway robbery.

My clever friend's work consists chiefly in reducing files of correspondence on a particular subject to one or two leading thoughts. Upon these he casts the colour of his own opinions, and submits the subjective product to the Secretary, or Member of Council, above him for final orders. His mind is one of the many refractive mediums through which Government looks out upon India.

From time to time he is called upon to write a minute, or a note, on some given subject, and then it is that his thoughts and words expand freely. He feels bound to cover an area of paper proportionate to his own opinion of his own importance; he feels bound to introduce a certain seasoning of foreign words and phrases; and he feels bound to create, if the occasion seems in any degree to warrant it, one of those cock-eyed, limping, stammering epigrams which belong exclusively to the official humour of Simla. I have said that the Secretary is clever, scornful, jocose, imperfectly sinful, and nimble with his pen. I shall only add that he has succeeded in catching the tone of the Imperial Bumbledom.

This tone is an affectation of æsthetic and literary sympathies, combined with a cynical disdain of everything Indian and Anglo-Indian. The flotsam and jetsam of advanced European thought are eagerly sought and treasured up. "The New Republic" is on every drawing-room table. One must speak of nothing but the latest doings at the Gaiety, the pictures of the last Academy, the ripest outcome of scepticism in the *Nineteenth Century*, or the aftermath in the *Fortnightly*. If I were to talk to our Secretariat man about the harvest prospects of the Deckan, the beauty of the Himalayan scenery, or the book I have just published in Calcutta about the Rent

Law, he would stare at me with feigned surprise and horror.

"When he thinks of his own native land
In a moment he seems to be there
But, alas! Ali Baba at hand
Soon hurries him back to despair.

No. VI.

H.E. THE BENGALI BABOO.

No. VI.

H.E. THE BENGALI BABOO.

THE ascidian that got itself evolved into Bengali Baboos must have seized the first moment of consciousness and thought to regret the step it had taken; for however much we may desire to diffuse Babooism over the Empire, we must all agree that the Baboo itself is a subject for tears.

The other day, as I was strolling down the Mall, whistling Beethoven's 9th Symphony, I met the Bengali Baboo. It was returning from office. I asked it if it had a soul. It replied that it had not; but that some day it hoped to pass the matriculation examination of the Calcutta University. I whistled the opening bars of one of Cherubini's Requiems, but I saw no resurrection in its eye; so I passed on.

When I was at Lhassa the Dalai Lama told me that a virtuous cow-hippopotamus by metempsychosis might, under unfavourable circumstances, become an undergraduate of the Calcutta University, and that, when patent-leather shoes and English supervened, the thing was a Baboo.

I forget whether it was the Duke of Buckingham, or Mr. Lethbridge, or General Scindia —I always mix up these C.I.E.'s together in my mind somehow—who told me that a Bengali Baboo had never been known to laugh, but only to giggle with clicking noises like a crocodile. Now this is very telling evidence; because if a baboo does not laugh at a C.I.E. he will laugh at nothing. The faculty must be wanting.

When Lord Macaulay said that what the milk was to the cocoa-nut, what beauty was to the buffalo, and what scandal was to woman, that Dr. Johnson's Dictionary was to the Bengali Baboo, he unquestionably spoke in terms of figurative exaggeration; neverthe-less a core of truth lies hidden in his remark. It is by the Baboo's words you know the Baboo. The true Baboo is full of words and phrases—full of inappropriate words and phrases lying about like dead men on a battle-field, in heaps, to be carted away promiscuously, without reference to kith or kin. You may turn on a Baboo at any moment and be quite sure that words, and phrases, and maxims, and proverbs will come gurgling forth, without reference to the subject or to the occasion, to what has gone before, or to what will come after. Perhaps it was with reference to this independence, buoyancy, and extravagance of language that Lord Lytton declared the Bengali to be "the Irishman of India."

You know, dear Vanity, I whispered to you before that the poor Baboo often suffers from a slight aberration of speech which prevents his articulating the truth—a kind of moral lisp. Lord Lytton could not have been alluding to this; for it was only yesterday that

I heard an Irishman speak the truth to Lord Lytton about some little matter—I forget what; cotton duty, I think—and Lord Lytton said, rather curtly, "Why, you have often told me this before." So Lord Lytton must be in the habit of hearing certain truths from the Irish.

It was either Sir Andrew Clarke, Sir Alexander Arbuthnot, or Sir Some-one-else, who understands all about these things, that first told me of the tendency to Baboo worship in England at present. I immediately took steps, when I heard of it, to capitalise my pension and purchase gold mines in the Wynaad and shares in the Simla Bank. (Colonel Peterson, of the Simla Fencibles, supported me gallantly in this latter resolution.) The notion of so dreadful a form of fetishism establishing itself in one's native land is repugnant to the feelings even of those who have been rendered callous to such things by seats in the Bengal Legislative Council.

Sir George Campbell took an interest in the development of the Baboo, and the selection of the fittest for Government employment. He taught them in debating-clubs the various modes of conducting irresponsible parliamentary chatter; and he tried to encourage pedestrianism and football to evolve their legs and bring them into something like harmony with their long pendant arms. You can still see a few of Sir George's leggy Baboos coiled up in corners of lecture-rooms at Calcutta. The Calcutta Cricket Club employs one as permanent "leg."

It is the future of Baboodom I tremble for. When they wax fat with new religions, music, painting, Comédie Anglaise, scientific discoveries, they may kick with those developed legs of theirs, until we shall have to think that they are something more than a joke, more than a mere *lusus naturæ*, more than a caricature moulded by the accretive and differentiating impulses of the monad in a moment of wanton playfulness. The fear is that their tendencies may infect others. The patent-leather shoes, the silk umbrellas, the ten-thousand horse-power English words and phrases, and the loose shadows of English thought, which are now so many Aunt Sallies for all the world to fling a jeer at, might among other races pass into dummy soldiers, and from dummy soldiers into trampling, hope-bestirred crowds, and so on, out of the province of Ali Baba and into the columns of serious reflection. Mr. Wordsworth and his friends the Dakhani Brahmans should consider how painful it would be, when deprived of the consolations of religion, to be solemnly repressed by the *Pioneer*—to be placed under that steam-hammer which by the descent of a paragraph can equally crack the tiniest of jokes and the hardest of political nuts, can suppress unauthorised inquiry and crush disaffection.

At present the Baboo is merely a grotesque Brocken shadow, but in the course of geological ages it might harden down into something palpable. It is this possibility that leads Sir Ashly Eden to advise the Baboo to revert to its original type. But it is not so easy to become homogeneous after you have been diluted with the physical sciences and stirred about by Positivists and missionaries. "I would I were a protoplastic monad!" may sound very rhythmical, poetical, and all that; but even for a Baboo the aspiration is not an easy one to gratify.

No. VII.

THE RAJA.

No. VII.

THE RAJA.

TRY not to laugh, Dear Vanity. I know you don't mean anything by it; but these Indian kings are so sensitive. The other day I was translating to a young Raja what Val Prinsep had said about him in his "Purple India." He had only said that he was a dissipated young ass and as ugly as a baboon; but the boy was quite hurt and began to cry. I had to send for the Political Agent to quiet him and put him to sleep. When you consider the matter philosophically there is nothing *per se* ridiculous in a Raja. Take a hypothetical case: picture to yourself a Raja who does not get drunk without some good reason, who is not ostentatiously unfaithful to his five-and-twenty queens and his five-and-twenty grand duchesses, who does not festoon his thorax and abdomen with curious cutlery and jewels, who does not paint his face with red ochre, and who sometimes takes a sidelong glance at his affairs, and there is no reason why you should not think of such a one as an Indian king. India is not very fastidious; so long as the Government is satisfied, the people of India do not much care what the Rajas are like. A peasant proprietor said to Mr. Caird and me the other day, "We are poor cultivators; we cannot afford to keep Rajas. The Rajas are for the Lord Sahib."

The young Maharaja of Kuch Parwani assures me that it is not considered the thing for a Raja at the present day to govern. "A really swell Raja amuses himself." One hoards money, another plays at soldiering, a third is horsey, a fourth is amorous, and a fifth gets drunk; at least so Kuch Parwani thinks. Please don't say that I told you this. The Foreign Secretary knows what a high opinion I have of the Rajas: indeed he often employs me to whitewash them when they get into scrapes. " A little playful, perhaps, but no more loyal Prince in India!" This is the kind of thing I put into the Annual Administration Reports of the Agencies, and I stick to it. Playful no doubt, but a more loyal class than the Rajas there is not in India. They have built their houses of cards on the thin crust of British Rule that now covers the crater, and they are ever ready to pour a pannikin of water into a crack to quench the explosive forces rumbling below.

The amiable chief in whose house I am staying to-day is exceedingly simple in his habits. At an early hour he issues from the zenana and joins two or three of his Thakores, or barons, who are on duty at Court, in the morning draught of opium. They sit in a circle, and a servant in the centre goes round and pours the *kasumbha* out of a brass bowl and through a woollen cloth into their hands, out of which they lap it up. Then a cardamum to take away the acrid after-taste. One hums drowsily two or three bars of an old-world song; another clears his throat and spits; the Chief yawns, and all snap their fingers, to prevent evil spirits skipping into his throat; a late riser joins the circle, and his fellow-courtiers give him *tazim*—that is, rise and salaam; a coarse jest or two, and the party disperses. A crowd of servants swarm round the Chief as he shuffles slowly away. Three or four mace-bearers walk in front shouting, "Umr, daulat ziyada ho." (May your age and wealth increase.) A confidential servant continually leans forward and whispers in his ear; another remains close at hand with a silver tea-pot containing water and wrapped up in a wet cloth to keep it cool; a third constantly whisks a yak's tail over the King's head; a fourth carries my Lord's sword; a fifth his handkerchief; and so on. Where is he going? He dawdles up a narrow staircase, through a dark corridor, down half a-dozen steep steps, across a courtyard overgrown with weeds, up another staircase, along another passage, and so to a range of heavy quilted red screens that conceal doors leading into the female penetralia. Here we must leave him. Two servants disappear behind the *parda* with their master, the others promptly lie down where they are, draw the sheets or blankets which they have been wearing over their faces and feet, and sleep.

About noon we see the King again. He is dressed in white flowing robes with a heavy carcanet of emeralds round his neck. His red turban is tied with strings of seed-pearls and set off with an aigrette springing from a diamond brooch. He sits on the Royal mattress, the *gáddi*. A big bolster covered with green velvet supports his back; his sword and shield are gracefully disposed before him. At the corner of the *gáddi* sits a little representation of himself in miniature, complete even to the sword and shield. This is his adopted son and heir. For all the queens and all the grand duchesses are childless, and a little kinsman had to be transplanted from a mud village among the cornfields to this dreamland palace to perpetuate the line. On the corners of the carpet on which the *gáddi* rests sit Thakores of the royal house, other Thakores sit below, right and left, forming two parallel lines, dwindling into Sardars, palace officers, and others of lower rank as they recede from the *gáddi*. Behind the Chief stand the servants with the emblems of royalty—the peacock feathers, the fan, the yak tail, and the umbrella (now furled). The confidential servant is still whispering into the ear of his master from time to time. This is durbar. No one speaks, unless to exchange a languid compliment with the Chief. Presently essence of roses and a compound of areca nut and lime are circulated: then a huge silver pipe is brought in, the Chief takes three long pulls, the Thakores on the carpet each take a pull, and the levée breaks up amid profound salaams. After this—dinner, opium, and sleep.

In the cool of the evening our King emerges from the palace, and, riding on a prodigiously fat white horse with pink points, proceeds to the place of carousal. A long train of horsemen follow him, and footmen run before with guns in red flannel covers and silver maces, shouting "Raja Maharaja salaamat," &c.

The horsemen immediately around him are mounted on well-fed and richly-caparisoned steeds, with all the bravery of cloth-of-gold, yak tails, silver chains, and strings of shells; behind are troopers in a burlesque of English uniform; and altogether in the rear is a mob of caitiffs on skeleton chargers, masquerading in every degree of shabbiness and rags, down to nakedness and a sword. The cavalcade passes through the city. The inhabitants pour out of every door and bend to the ground. Red cloths and white veils flutter at the casements overhead. You would hardly think that the spectacle was one daily enjoyed by the city. There is all the hurrying and eagerness of novelty and curiosity. Here and there a little shy crowd of women gather at a door and salute the Chief with a loud, shrill verse of discordant song. It is some national song of the Chief's ancestors and of the old heroic days. The place of carousal is a bare spot near a large and ancient well out of which grows a vast pipal-tree. Hard by is a little temple surmounted by a red flag on a drooping bamboo. It is here that the *Gangór* and *Dassahra* solemnities are celebrated. Arrived on the ground, the Raja slowly circles his horse; then, jerking the thorn-bit, causes him to advance plunging and rearing, but dropping first on the near foot and then on the off foot with admirable precision; and finally, making the white monster, now in a lather of sweat, rise up and walk a few steps on his hind legs, the Raja's performance concludes amid many shouts of wonder and delight from the smooth-tongued courtiers. The Thakores and Sardars now exhibit their skill in the *manège* until the shades of night fall, when torches are brought, amid much salaaming, and the cavalcade defiles, through the city, back to the palace. Lights are twinkling from the higher casements and reflected on the lake below; the *gola* slave-girls are singing plaintive songs; drum and conch answer from the open court-yards. The palace is awake. The Raja, we will romantically presume, bounds lightly from his horse, and dances gaily to the harem to fling himself voluptuously into the luxurious arms of one of the five-and-twenty queens, or one of the five-and-twenty grand duchesses;

and they stand for one delirious moment wreathed in each other's embraces—

> While soft there breathes
> Through the cool casement, mingled with the sighs
> Of moonlight flowers, music that seems to rise
> From some still lake, so liquidly it rose,
> And, as it swell'd again at each faint close,
> The ear could track through all that maze of chords
> And young sweet voices these impassioned words—

"Ho, you there! fetch us a pint of gin! and look sharp, will you!"

> For who, in time, knows whither we may vent
> The treasure of our tongue, to what strange shores
> This gain of our best glory shall be sent,
> To enrich unknowing nations with our stores!
> What worlds in the yet unformed Orient
> May come refined with accents that are ours!

But, dear Vanity, I can see that you are impatient of scenes whose luxuries steal, spite of yourself, too deep into your soul; besides, I dread the effect of such warm situations on a certain Zuleika to whom the note of Ali Baba is like the thrice-distilled strains of the bulbul on Bendemeer's stream. So let us electrify ourselves back to prose and propriety by thinking of the Political Agent. Let us plunge into the cold waters of dreary reality by conjuring up a figure in tail-coat and gold buttons dispensing justice while H.H. the romantic and picturesque Raja, G.C.S.I., amuses himself. Yet we hear cries from the gallery of "Vive M. le Raja; vive la bagatelle!"

So say we, in faint echoes, defying the anathemas of the Foreign Office. Do not turn this beautiful temple of ancient days into a mere mill for decrees and budgets; but sweep it and purify it, and render it a fitting shrine for the homage and tribute of antique loyalty—"that proud submission, that subordination of the heart which kept alive, even in servitude itself, the spirit of an exalted freedom." With tail-coat and cocked-hat government "the unbought grace of life, the cheap defence of nations, the nurse of manly sentiment and heroic enterprise is gone."

No. VIII.

THE POLITICAL AGENT,

A MAN IN BUCKRAM.

No. VIII.

THE POLITICAL AGENT,

A MAN IN BUCKRAM.

THIS is a most curious product of the Indian bureaucracy. Nothing in all White Baboodom is so wonderful as the Political Agent. A near relation of the Empress who was travelling a good deal about India some three or four years ago said that he would rather get a Political Agent, with raja, chuprassies, and everything complete, to take home, than the unfigured "mum" of Beluchistan, or the sea-aye-ee mocking bird, *Kokiolliensis Lyt-*

tonia. But the Political Agent cannot be taken home. The purple bloom fades in the scornful climate of England; the paralytic swagger passes into sheer imbecility; the thirteen-gun tall-talk reverberates in jeering echoes; the chuprassies are only so many black men, and the raja is felt to be a joke. The Political Agent cannot live beyond Aden.

The Government of India keeps its Political Agents scattered over the native states in small jungle stations. It furnishes them with maharajas, nawabs, rajas, and chuprassies, according to their rank, and it usually throws in a house, a gaol, a doctor, a volume of Aitchison's Treaties, an escort of native Cavalry, a Star of India, an assistant, the powers of a first-class magistrate, a flag-staff, six camels, three tents, and a salute of eleven or thirteen guns. In very many cases the Government of India nominates a Political Agent to the rank of Son-to-a-Lieut.-Governor, Son-in-Law-to-a-Lieut.-Governor, Son-to-a-Member-of-Council, or Son-to-an-Agent-to-the-Governor-General. Those who are thus elevated to the Anglo-Indian peerage need have no thought for the morrow, what they shall do, what they shall say, or wherewithal they shall be supplied with a knowledge of oriental language and occidental law. Nature clothes them with increasing quantities of gold lace and starry ornaments, and that charming, if unblushing, female—Lord Lytton begs me to write "maid"—Miss Anglo-Indian Promotion, goes skipping about among them like a joyful kangaroo.

The Politicals are a Greek chorus in our popular burlesque, "Empire." The Foreign Secretary is the prompter. The company is composed of nawabs and rajahs (with the Duke of Buckingham as a "super"). Lord Meredith is the scene-shifter; Sir John, the manager. The Secretary of State, with his council, is in the stage-box; the House of Commons in the stalls; the London Press in the gallery; the East Indian Association, Exeter Hall, Professor Fawcett, Mr. Hyndman, and the criminal classes generally, in the pit; while those naughty little Scotch boys, the shock-headed Duke and Monty Duff, who once tried to turn down the lights, pervade the house with a policeman on their horizon. As we enter the theatre a dozen chiefs are dancing in the ballet to express their joy at the termination of the Afghan War. The political *choreutæ* are clapping their hands, encouraging them by name and pointing them out to the gallery.

The government of a native state by clerks and chuprassies, with a beautiful *fainéant* Political Agent for Sundays and Hindu festivals, is, I am told, a thing of the past. Colonel Henderson, the imperial "Peeler," tells me so, and he ought to know, for he is a kind of demi-official superintendent of Thugs and Agents. Nowadays, my informant assures me, the Political Agents undergo a regular training in a Madras Cavalry Regiment, or in the Central India Horse, or on the Viceroy's Staff, and if they have to take charge of a Mahratta State they are obliged to pass an examination in classical Persian poetry. This is as it ought to be. The intricacies of Oriental intrigue and the manifold complication of tenure and revenue that entangle administrative procedure in the protected principalities, will unravel themselves in presence of men who have enjoyed such advantages.

When I first came out to this country I was placed in charge of three degrees of latitude and eight of longitude in Rajputana that I might learn the language. The soil was sandy, the tenure feudal (*zabardast*, as we call it in India), and the Raja a lunatic by nature and a dipsomaniac by education. He had been educated by his grandmamma and the hereditary Minister. I found that his grandmamma and the hereditary Minister were most anxious to relieve me of the most embarrassing details of Government, so I handed them a copy of the Ten Commandments, underlining two that I thought might be useful, and put them in charge. They were old-fashioned in their methods—like Sir Billy Jones; but their results were admirable. In two years the revenue was reduced from ten to two lakhs of rupees, and the expenditure proportionately increased. A bridge, a summer-house, and a school were built; and I wrote the longest "Administration Report" that has ever issued from the Zulmabad Residency. When I left money was so cheap and lightly regarded that I sold my old buggy horse for two thousand rupees to grandmamma, with many mutual expressions of good-will—through a curtain—and I have not been paid to this day. But since then the horse-market has been ruined in the native states by these imperial *mêlas* and durbars. A poor Political has no chance against these Government-of-India people, who come down with strings of three-legged horses, and—no, I won't say they sell them to the chiefs—I should be having a commission of my *khidmatgars* sitting upon me, like poor Har Sahai, who was beaten by Mr. Saunders, and Malhar Rao Gaikwar, who fancied his Resident was going to poison him.

I like to see a Political up at Simla wooing that hoyden Promotion in her own sequestered bower. It is good to see Hercules toiling at the feet of Omphale. It is good to see Pistol fed upon leeks by Under-Secretaries and women. How simple he is! How boyish he can be, and yet how intense! He will play leap frog at Annandale; he will paddle about in the stream below the water-falls without shoes and stockings; but if you allude in the most distant way to rajas or durbars, he lets down his face a couple of holes and talks like a weather prophet. He will be so interesting that you can hardly bear it; so interesting that you will feel sorry he is not talking to the Governor-General up at Peterhoff.

No. IX.

THE COLLECTOR.

No. IX.

THE COLLECTOR.

WAS it not the Bishop of Bombay who said that man was an automaton plus the mirror of consciousness? The Government of every Indian province is an automaton plus the mirror of consciousness. The Secretariat is consciousness, and the Collectors form the automaton. The Collector works, and the Secretariat observes and registers.

To the people of India the Collector is the Imperial Government. He watches over their welfare in the many facets which reflect our civilisation. He establishes schools, dispensaries, gaols, and courts of justice. He levies the rent of their fields, he fixes the tariff, and he nominates to every appointment, from that of road-sweeper, or constable, to the great blood-sucking offices round the Court and Treasury. As for Boards of Revenue and Lieutenant-Governors who occasionally come sweeping across the country, with their locust hosts of servants and petty officials, they are but an occasional nightmare; while the Governor-General is a mere shadow in the background of thought, half blended with "John Company Bahadur" and other myths of the dawn.

The Collector lives in a long rambling bungalow furnished with folding chairs and tables, and in every way marked by the provisional arrangements of camp life. He seems to have just arrived from out of the firmament of green fields and mango groves that encircles the little station where he lives; or he seems just about to pass away into it again. The shooting-howdahs are lying in the verandah, the elephant of a neighbouring landholder is swinging his hind foot to and fro under a tree, or switching up straw and leaves on to his back, a dozen camels are lying down in a circle making bubbling noises, and tents are pitched here and there to dry, like so many white wings on which the whole establishment is about to rise and fly away—fly away into "the district," which is the correct expression for the vast expanse of level plain melting into blue sky on the wide horizon-circle around.

The Collector is a bustling man. He is always in a hurry. His multitudinous duties succeed one another so fast that one is never ended before the next begins. A mysterious thing called "the Joint" comes gleaning after him, I believe, and completes the inchoate work.

The verandah is full of fat black men in clean linen waiting for interviews. They are bankers, shopkeepers, and landowners, who have only come to "pay their respects," with ever so little a petition as a corollary. The chuprassie-vultures hover about them. Each of these obscene fowls has received a gratification from each of the clean fat men; else the clean fat men would not be in the verandah. This import tax is a wholesome restraint upon the excessive visiting tendencies of wealthy men of colour. Brass dishes filled with pistachio nuts and candied sugar are ostentatiously displayed here and there; they are the oblations of the would-be visitors. The English call these offerings "dollies"; the natives *dáli.* They represent in the profuse East the visiting cards of the meagre West.

Although from our lofty point of observation, among the pine-trees, the Collector seems to be of the smallest social calibre, a mere carronade, not to be distinguished by any proper name; in his own district he is a Woolwich Infant; and a little community of microscopicals,—doctors, engineers, inspectors of schools, and assistant magistrates, look up to him as to a magnate.

They tell little stories of his weaknesses and eccentricities, and his wife is considered a person entitled "to give herself airs" (within the district) if she feels so disposed; while to their high dinners is allowed the use of champagne and "Europe" talk on æsthetic subjects. The Collector is not, however, permitted to wear a chimney-pot hat and gloves on Sunday (unless he has been in the Provincial Secretariat as a boy); a Terai hat is sufficient for a Collector.

A Collector is usually a sportsman; when he is a poet, a co-respondent, or a neologist it is thought rather a pity; and he is spoken of in undertones. Neology is considered especially reprehensible. The junior member of the Board of Revenue, or even the commissioner of a division (if he be *pakka*), may question the literal inspiration of Genesis; but it is not good form for a Collector to tamper with his Bible. A Collector should have no leisure for opinions of any sort.

I have said that a Collector is usually a sportsman. In this capacity he is frequently made use of by the Viceroy and 'long-shore Governors, as he is an adept at showing sport to globe-trotters. The villagers who live on the borders of the jungle will generally turn out and beat for the Collector; and the petty chief who owns the jungle always keeps a tiger or two for district officers. A Political Agent's tiger is known to be a domestic animal suitable for delicate noble lords travelling for health; but a Collector's tiger is often a wild beast, although reared upon buffalo calves and accustomed to be driven. The Collector, who is always the most unselfish and hospitable of men, only kills the fatted tiger for persons of distinction with letters of introduction. Any common jungle tiger, even a man-eater, is good enough for himself and his friends.

The Collector never ventures to approach Simla, when on leave. At Simla people would stare and raise their eye-brows if they heard that a Collector was on the hill. They would ask what sort of a thing a Collector was. The Press Commissioner would be sent to interview it. The children at Peterhoff would send for it to play with. So the clodhopping Collector goes to Naini Tal or Darjiling, where he is known either as Ellenborough Higgins, or Higgins of Gharibpur, in territorial fashion. Here he is understood. Here he can babble of his *Bandobast*, his *Balbacha* and his *Bawarchikhana* ; and here he can speak in familiar accents of his neighbours, Dalhousie Smith and Cornwallis Jones. All day long he strides up and down the club verandah with his old Haileybury chum, Teignmouth Tompkins;

and they compare experiences of the hunting-field and office, and denounce in unmeasured terms of Oriental vituperation the new sort of civilian who moves about with the Penal Code under his arm and measures his authority by statute, clause, and section.

In England the Collector is to be found riding at anchor in the Bandicoot Club. He makes two or three hurried cruises to his native village, where he finds himself half forgotten. This sours him. The climate seems worse than of old, the means of locomotion at his disposal are inconvenient and expensive; he yearns for the sunshine and elephants of Gharibpur; and returns, an older and a quieter man.

The afternoon of life is throwing longer shadows, the Acheron of promotion is gaping before him; he falls into a Commissionership; still deeper into an officiating seat on the Board of Revenue. *Facilis est decensus, etc.* Nothing will save him now; transmigration has set in; the gates of Simla fly open; it is all over. Let us pray that his halo may fit him.

No. X.

BABY IN PARTIBUS.

No. X.

BABY IN PARTIBUS.

THE Empire has done less for Anglo-Indian Babies than for any class of the great exile community. Legislation provides them with neither rattle nor coral, privilege leave nor pension. Papa has a Raja and Star of India to play with; Mamma the Warrant of Precedence and the Hill Captains; but Baby has nothing—not even a missionary; Baby is without the amusement of the meanest cannibal.

Baby is debarred from the society of his

compatriots. His father is cramped and frozen with the chill cares of office; his mother is deadened by the gloomy routine of economy and fashion; custom lies upon her with a weight heavy as frost and deep almost as life; the fountains of natural fancy and mirth are frozen over; so Baby lisps his dawn pæans in soft Oriental accents, wakening harmonious echoes among those impulsive and impressionable children of Nature who masque themselves in the black slough of Bearers and Ayahs; and Baby blubbers in Hindustani.

The Ayah and Bearer sit with Baby in the verandah on a little carpet; broken toys and withered flowers lie around. They croon to baby some old-world *katabaukalesis*; while beauty, born of murmuring sound, passes into Baby's eyes. The squirrel sits chirruping familiarly on the edge of the verandah with his tail in the air and some uncracked pericarp in his uplifted hands, the kite circles aloft and whistles a shrill and mournful note, the sparrows chatter, the crow clears his throat, the minas scream discordantly, and Baby's soft, receptive nature thus absorbs an Indian language.

Very soon Baby will think from right to left, and will lisp in the luxuriant bloom of Oriental hyperbole.

In the evening Baby will go out for an airing with the Bearer and Ayah, and while they dawdle along the dusty road, or sit on kerb-stones and on culvert parapets, he will listen to the extensile tale of their simple sorrows. He will hear, with a sigh, that the profits of petty larceny are declining; he will be taught to regret the increasing infirmities of his Papa's temper; and portraits in sepia of his Mamma will be observed by him to excite laughter mingled with dark impulsive words. Thus there will pass into Baby's eyes glances of suspicious questionings, "the blank misgivings of a creature moving about in worlds not realised."

In the long summer days Baby will patter listlessly about the darkened rooms accompanied by his suite, who carry a feeding bottle —Maw's Patent Feeding Bottle—just as the Sergeant-at-Arms carries the mace; and, from time to time, little Mister Speaker will squat down on his dear little hams and take a refreshing pull or two At breakfast and luncheon little Mister Speaker will straggle into the dining-room, and fond parents will give him a tid-bit of many soft dainties, to be washed down with brandy and water, beer, sherry, or other alcoholic draught. On such broken meals Baby is raised.

The little drawn face, etiolated and weary-looking, recommends sleep; but Baby is a bad sleeper. The Bearer-in-waiting carries about a small pillow all day long, and from time to time Baby is applied to it. He frets and cries, and they brood over him, humming some plaintive Indian lullaby. Still he turns restlessly and whimpers, though they pat him and shampoo him, and call him fond names, and tell him soothing stories of bulbuls and flowers and woolly sheep. But Baby does not sleep, and even Indian patience is exhausted. Both Ayah and Bearer would like to slip away to their mud houses at the other end of the compound and have a pull at the fragrant *huqqa* and a gossip with the *saices*; but while *Sunny Baba* is at large, and might at any moment make a raid on Mamma, who is dozing over a novel on a spider-chair near the mouth of the thermantidote, the Ayah and Bearer dare not leave their charge. So *Sunny Baba* must sleep, and the Bearer has in the folds of his waist-cloth a little black fragment of the awful sleep-compeller, and Baby is drugged into a deep uneasy sleep of delirious, racking dreams.

Day by day baby grows paler, day by day thinner, day by day a stranger light burns in his bonny eyes. Weird thoughts sweep through Baby's brain, weird questions startle Mamma out of the golden languors in which she is steeped, weird words frighten the gentle Ayah as she fondles her darling. The current of babble and laughter has almost ceased to flow. Baby lies silent in the Ayah's lap staring at the ceiling. He clasps a broken toy with wasted fingers. His Bearer comes with some old watchword of fun; Baby smiles faintly, but makes no response. The old man takes him tenderly in his arms and carries him to the verandah; Baby's head falls heavily on his shoulder.

The outer world lies dimly round Baby; within, strange shadows are flitting by. The wee body is pressing heavily upon the spirit; Baby is becoming conscious of the burthen. He will be quiet for hours on his little cot; he does not sleep, but he dreams. Earth's joys and lights are fast fading out of those resilient eyes; Baby's spirit is waiting on the shores of eternity, and already hears "the mighty waters rolling evermore."

The broken toys are swept away into a corner: a silence and fear have fallen upon the household, black servants weep, their mistress seeks refuge in headache and smelling-salts: the hard father feels a strange, an irrepressible welling up of little memories. He loves the golden-haired boy; he hardly knew it before. If he could only hear once more the merry laugh, the chatter, and the shouting! But he cannot hear it any more; he will never hear his child's voice again. Baby has passed into the far-away Thought-World. Baby is now only a dream and a memory, only the recollection of a music that is heard no more. Baby has crossed that cloudy, storm-driven bourn of speculation and fear whither we are all tending.

"A few white bones upon a lonely sand,
A rotting corpse beneath the meadow grass,
That cannot hear the footsteps as they pass,
Memorial urns pressed by some foolish hand
Have been for all the goal of troublous fears,
Ah! breaking hearts and faint eyes dim with tears,
And momentary hope by breezes fanned
To flame that ever fading falls again,
And leaves but blacker night and deeper pain,
Have been the mould of life in every land."

Baby is planted out for evermore in the dank and weedy little cemetery that lies on the outskirts of the station where he lived and died. Those golden curls, those soft and rounded limbs, and that laughing mouth, are given up to darkness and the eternal hunger of corruption. Through sunshine and rain, through the long days of summer, through the long nights of winter, for ever, for ever, Baby lies silent and dreamless under that waving grass. The bee will hum overhead for evermore, and the swallow glance among the cypress. The butterfly will flutter for ages and ages among the rank flowers—Baby will still lie there. Come away, come away, your cheeks are pale, it cannot be, we cannot believe it, we must not remember it; other Baby voices will re-kindle our life and love, Baby's toys will pass to other Baby hands. All will change; we will change.

> "Yet, darling, but come back to me,
> Whatever change the years have wrought,
> I find not yet one lonely thought
> That cries against my wish for thee."

No. XI.

THE RED CHUPRASSIE;

OR, THE CORRUPT LICTOR.

No. XI.

THE RED CHUPRASSIE;

OR, THE CORRUPT LICTOR.*

The red chuprassie is our Colorado beetle, our potato disease, our Home Ruler, our cupboard skeleton, the little rift in our lute. The red-coated chuprassie is a cancer in our Administration. To be rid of it there is hardly any surgical operation we would not cheerfully undergo. You might extract the

---

* The chuprassies are official messengers, wearing Imperial livery, who are attached to civil officers in India.

Bishop of Bombay, amputate the Governor of Madras, put a seton in the pay and allowances of the Lieutenant-Governor of Bengal, and we should smile.

The red chuprassie is ubiquitous; he is in the verandah of every official's house in India, from that of the Governor-General downwards; he is in the portico of every Court of Justice, every Treasury, every Public Office, every Government School, every Government Dispensary in the country. He walks behind the Collector; he follows the conservancy carts; he prowls about the candidate for employment; he hovers over the accused and accuser; he haunts the Raja; he infests the tax-payer.

He wears the Imperial livery; he is to the entire population of India the exponent of British Rule; he is the mother-in-law of liars, the high-priest of extortioners, and the receiver-general of bribes.

Through this refracting medium the people of India see their rulers. The chuprassie paints his master in colours drawn from his own black heart. Every lie he tells, every insinuation he throws out, every demand he makes, is endorsed with his master's name. He is the arch-slanderer of our name in India.

There is no city in India, no mofussil-station, no little settlement of officials far-up country, in which the chuprassie does not find sworn brothers and confederates. The cutcherry clerks and the police are with him everywhere; higher native officials are often on his side.

He sits at the receipt of custom in the Collector's verandah, and no native visitor dare approach who has not conciliated him with money. The candidate for employment, educated in our schools, and pregnant with words about purity, equality, justice, political economy, and all the rest of it, addresses him with joined hands as "Maharaj," and slips silver into his itching palm. The successful place-hunter pays him a feudal relief on receiving office or promotion, and benevolences flow in from all who have anything to hope or fear from those in power.

In the Native States the chuprassie flourishes rampantly. He receives a regular salary, through their representatives or vakıls at the agencies, from all the native chiefs round about, and on all occasions of visits or return visits, durbars, religious festivals, or public ceremonials, he claims and receives preposterous fees. The Rajas, whose dignity is always exceedingly delicate, stand in great fear of the chuprassies. They believe that on public occasions the chuprassies have sometimes the power of sicklying them o'er with the pale cast of neglect.

English officers who have become de-Europeanised from long residence among natives, or by the frequent performance of petty ceremonial duties of an Oriental hue, employ chuprassies to aggrandise their importance. They always figure on a background of red chuprassies. Such officials are what Lord Lytton calls " White Baboos."

A great Maharaja once told me that it was the tyranny of the Government chuprassies that made him take to drink. He spoke of them as "the Pindarries of modern India." He had a theory that the small pay we gave them accounted for their evil courses. (A chuprassie gets about eight pounds sterling a year.) He added that if we saw a chuprassie on seven rupees a month living overtly at the rate of a thousand, we ought immediately to appoint him an *attaché*, or put him in gaol.

I make a simple rule in my own establishment of dismissing a chuprassie as soon as he begins to wax fat. A native cannot become rich without waxing fat, because wealth is primarily enjoyed by the mild Gentoo as a means of procuring greasy food in large quantities. His secondary enjoyment is to sit upon it. He digs a hole in the ground for his rupees, and broods over them, like a great obscene fowl. If you see a native sitting very hard on the same place day after day, you will find it worth your while to dig him up. Shares in this are better than the Madras gold mines.

In early Company days, when the Empire was a baby, the European writers regarded with a kindly eye those profuse Orientals who went about bearing gifts; but Lord Clive closed this branch of the business, and it has been taken up by our scarlet-runners, or verandah parasites, in our name. Now, dear

Vanity, you may call me a Russophile, or by any other marine term of endearment you like, if I don't think the old plan were the better of the two. We ourselves could conduct corruption decently; but to be responsible for corruption over which we exercise no control is to lose the credit of a good name and the profits of a bad one.

I hear that the Government of India proposes to form a mixed committee of Rajas and chuprassies to discuss the question as to whether native chiefs ever give bribes and native servants ever take them. It is expected that a report favourable to Indian morality will be the result. Of course Raja Joe Hookham will preside.

No. XII.

THE PLANTER;

A FARMER PRINCE.

No. XII.

THE PLANTER;

A FARMER PRINCE.

THE Planter lives to-day as we all lived fifty years ago. He lives in state and bounty, like the Lord of Burleigh. He lives like that fine old English gentleman who had an old estate, and who kept up his old mansion at a bountiful old rate. He lives in a grand wholesale manner; he lives in round numbers; he lives like a hero. Everything is Homeric about him. He establishes himself firmly in the land with great joy and plenty; and he gathers round him all that makes life full-toned and harmonious, from the grand timbre of draught-ale and the organ-thunder of hunting, to the piccolo and tintinnabulum of Poker and maraschino. His life is a fresco-painting, on which some Cyclopæan Raphaelite has poured his rainbows from a fire-engine of a hundred-elephant power.

We paltry officials live meanly in pen-and-ink sketches. Our little life is rounded by a dream of promotion and pension. We toil, we slave; we put by money, we pinch ourselves. We are hardly fit to live in this beautiful world, with its laughing girls and grapes, its summer seas, its sunshine and flowers, its Garnet Wolseleys and bulbuls. We go moping through its glories in green spectacles, befouling it with our loathsome statistics and reports. The sweet air of heaven, the blue firmament, and the everlasting hills do not satisfy our poisoned hearts; so we make to ourselves a little tin-pot world of blotted-paper, debased rupees, graded lists, and tinsel honours; we try to feed our lungs on its typhoidal effluvia. Aroint thee, Comptroller and Accountant-

General, with all thy griesly crew! Thou art worse than the blind Fury with the abhorred shears; for thou slittest my thin-spun-pay wearing spectacles, thrice branded varlet!

Dear Vanity, of course you understand that I do not allude to the amiable old gentleman who controls our Accounts Department, who is the mirror of tenderness. The person I would impale is a creation of my own wrath, a mere official type struck in frenzied fancy.

Let us soothe ourselves by contemplating the Planter and his generous, simple life. It calms one to look at him. He is something placid, strong, and easeful. Without wishing to appear obsequious, I always feel disposed to borrow money when I meet a substantial Planter. He inspires confidence. I grasp his strong hand; I take him (figuratively) to my heart, while the desire to bank with him wells up mysteriously in my bosom.

He lives in a grand old bungalow, surrounded by ancient trees. Large rooms open upon one another on every side in long vistas; a broad and hospitable-looking verandah girds all. Everywhere trophies of the chase meet the eye. We walk upon cool matting; we recline upon long-armed chairs; low and heavy punkahs swing overhead; a sweet breathing of wet *khaskhas* grass comes sobbing out of the thermantidote; and a gigantic, but gentle, *khidmatgar* is always at our elbow with long glasses on a silver tray. This man's name is Nubby Bux, but he means nothing by it, and a child might play with him. I often say to him in a caressing tone "*Peg lao*"; and he is grateful for any little attention of this sort.

It is near noon. My friend Mr. Great-Heart, familiarly known as "Jamie Macdonald," has been taking me over the factory and stables. We have been out since early morning on the jumpiest and beaniest of Waler mares. I am not killed, but a good deal shaken. The glass trembles in my hand. I have an absorbing thirst, and I drink copiously, almost passionately. My outstretched legs are reposing on the arms of my chair and I stiffen into an attitude of rest. I hear my host splashing and singing in his tub.

Breakfast is a meal conceived in a large

and liberal spirit. We pass from dish to dish through all the compass of a banquet, the diapason closing full in beer. Several joyful assistants, whose appetites would take first-class honours at any cattle show, join the hunt and are well in at the beer. What tales are told! I feel glad that Mrs. Mary Somerville and Dr. Watts are not present. I keep looking round to see that no bishop comes into the room. It is a comfort to me to think that Bishop Heber is dead. I gave up blushing five years ago when I entered the Secretariat; but if at this moment Sir William Jones were to enter, or Mr. Whitley Stokes with his child-like heart and his Cymric vocabulary, I believe I should be strangely affected.

The day welters on through drink and billiards. In the afternoon more joyful Planters drop in, and we play a rubber. From whist to the polo ground, where I see the merry men of Tirhoot play the best and fastest game that the world can show. At night high carousals and potations pottle deep. Next morning sees the entire party in the *khadar* of the river, mounted on Arabs, armed with spears, hunting Jamie Macdonald's Calydonian boar. These Scotchmen never forget their nationality.

And while these joyful Planters are thus rejoicing, the indigo is growing silently all round. While they play, Nature works for them. So does the patient black man; he smokes his *huqqa* and keeps an eye on the rising crop.

You will have learnt from Mr. Caird that indigo grows in cakes (the ale is imported); to his description of the process of manufacture I can only add that the juice is generally expressed in the vernacular. You give a cake of the raw material to a coloured servant, you stand over him to see that he doesn't eat it, and your assistant canes him slowly as he squeezes the juice into a blue bottle. Blue pills are made of the refuse; your female servants use aniline dyes; and there you are. If any one dies in any other way you can refuse him the rites of cremation; fine him four annas; and warn him not to do it again. This is a burning question in Tirhoot and occasions much litigation.

Jamie Macdonald has now a contract for dyeing the blue ribbons of the turf; Tommy Begg has taken the blue boars and the Oxford Blues; and Bobby Thomas does the blue-books and the True Blues. It may not be generally known that the aristocracy do not employ aniline dyes for their blue blood. The minor Planters do business chiefly in blue stockings, blue bonnets, blue bottles, blue beards, and blue coats. For more information of this kind I can only refer you to Mr. Caird and the *Nineteenth Century*.

Some Planters grow tea, coffee, lac, mother-of-pearl, pickles, poppadums and curry powder —but now I am becoming encyclopædic and scientific, and trespassing on ground already taken up by the Famine Commission.

Fewer Planters are killed now by the wild camels who roam over the mango fields, but a good deal of damage is still done to the prickly pear trees. Mr. Cunningham has written an interesting note on this. Rewards have still to be offered for dead tigers and persons who have died of starvation. "When the

Government will not give a doit to relieve a lame beggar, they will lay out ten to see a dead Indian."

No. XIII.

THE EURASIAN;

A STUDY IN CHIARO-OSCURO.

No. XIII.

THE EURASIAN;

STUDY IN CHIARO-OSCURO.

THE Anglo-Indian has a very fine eye for colour. He will mark down "one anna in the rupee" with unerring certainty; he will suspect smaller coin. He will tell you how he can detect an adulterated European by his knuckles, his nails, his eyebrows, his pronunciation of the vowels, and his conception of propriety in dress, manner, and conduct.

To the thoroughbred Anglo-Indian, whose blood has distilled through Haileybury for three generations, and whose cousins to the fourth degree are Collectors and Indian Army Colonels, the Eurasian, however fair he may be, is a *bête noir*. Mrs. Ellenborough Higgins is always setting, or pointing at black blood.

And sometimes the whitey-brown man is objectionable. He is vain, apt to take offence, sly, indolent, sensuous; and, like Reuben, "unstable as water." He has a facile smile, a clammy hand, a manner either forward or obsequious, a mincing gait, and not always the snowiest linen.

Towards natives the Eurasian is cold, haughty, and formal; and this attitude is repaid, with interest, in scorn and hatred. There is no concealing the fact that to the mild Gentoo the Eurasian is a very distasteful object.

But having said this, the case for the prosecution closes, and we may turn to the many soft and gentle graces which the Eurasian developes.

In all the relations of family life the Eurasian is admirable. He is a dutiful son, a circumspect husband, and an affectionate father. He seldom runs through a fortune; he hardly ever elopes with a young lady of fashion; he is not in the habit of cutting off his son with a shilling; and he is an infrequent worshipper in that Temple of Separation where *Decrees Nisi* sever the Gordian knots of Hymen.

As a citizen he is zealously loyal. He will speak at municipal meetings, write letters about drainage and conservancy to the papers, observe local holidays in his best clothes, and attend funerals.

The Eurasian is a methodical and trustworthy clerk, and often occupies a position of great trust and responsibility in our public offices. He is not bold or original, like Sir Andrew Clerk; or amusing, like Mr. Stokes; but he does what work is given him to do without overstepping the modesty of nature

The Eurasian girl is often pretty and graceful; and, if the solution of India in her veins be weak, there is an unconventionality and *naïveté* sometimes which undoubtedly has a charm; and which, my dear friend, J. H——, of the 110th Clodhoppers (Lord Cardwell's

Own Clodhoppers) never could resist: "What though upon her lips there hung the accents of the tchi-tchi tongue."

A good many Eurasians who are not clerks in public offices, or telegraph signallers, or merchants, are loafers. They are passed on wherever they are found, to the next station, and thus they are kept in healthy circulation throughout India. They are all in search of employment on the railway; but as a provisional arrangement, to meet the more immediate and pressing exigencies of life, they will accept a small gratuity. They are mainly supported by municipalities, who keep them in brandy, rice, and railway-tickets out of funds raised for this purpose. Workhouses and Malacca canes have still to be tried.

Bishop Gell's plan for colonising the Laccadives and Cocos with these loafers has not met with much acceptance at Simla. The Home Secretary does not see from what Imperial fund they can be supplied with bathing drawers and barrel organs; but the Home Secretary ought to know that there is a philanthropic society at Lucknow of the disinterested, romantic, Turnerelli type, ready to furnish all the wants of a young colony, from under-clothing to Eno's fruit salt.

A great many wise proposals emanate from Simla as regards some artificial future for the Eurasian. One Ten-thousand-pounder asks Creation in a petulant tone of surprise why Creation does not make the Eurasian a carpenter; another looks round the windy hills and wonders why somebody does not make the Eurasian a high farmer. The shovel-hats are surprised that the Eurasian does not become a missionary, or a schoolmaster, or a policeman, or something of that sort. The native papers say, "Deport him"; the white prints say, "Make him a soldier"; and the Eurasian himself says, "Make me a Commissioner, or give me a pension." In the meantime, while nothing is being done, we can rail at the Eurasian for not being as we are.

> "Let us sit on the thrones
> In a purple sublimity,
> And grind down men's bones
> To a pale unanimity."

There is no proper classification of the

mixed race in India as there is in America. The convenient term *quadroon*, for instance, instead of "four annas in the rupee," is quite unknown; the consequence is that everyone —from Anna Maria De Souza, the "Portuguese" cook, a nobleman on whose cheek the best shoe-blacking would leave a white mark, to pretty Miss Fitzalan Courtney, of the Bombay Fencibles, who is as white as an Italian princess—is called an "Eurasian."

Do you know, dear Vanity, that it is not impossible that King Asoka (of the Edict Pillars), the "Constantine of Buddhism," was an Eurasian. I have not got the works of Arrian, or Mr. Leithbridge's "History of the World" at hand, but I have some recollection of Sandracottus, or one of Asoka's fathers or grandfathers, marrying a Miss Megasthenes, or Seleucus. With such memories, no wonder they call us "Mean Whites."

No. XIV.

THE VILLAGER.

No. XIV.

THE VILLAGER.

"Venio nunc ad voluptates agricolarum, quibus ego" (like the Famine Commissioners) "incredibiliter delector."

I MISSED two people at the Delhi Assemblage of 1877. All the gram-fed secretaries and most of the alcoholic chiefs were there; but the famine-haunted villager and the delirium-shattered, opium-eating Chinaman, who had to pay the bill, were not present.

I cannot understand why Viceroys and English newspapers call the Indian cultivator "riot." He never amounts to a riot if you treat him properly. He may be a disorderly crowd sometimes; but that is only when you embody him in a police force or convert him into cavalry. The atomic disembodied villager has no notion of rioting, *ça-ira* singing, or any of the tomfooleries of revolution. These pastimes are for men who are both idle and frivolous. When our villager wants to realise a political idea, he dies of famine. This has about it a certain air of seriousness. A man will not die of famine unless he be in earnest.

Lord Bacon's apothegm was that *Eating maketh a full man;* and it would be better to give the starving cultivator Bacon than the report of that Commission (which we cannot name without tears and laughter) which goes to work on the assumption that *writing maketh a full man*—that to write over a certain area of paper will fill the collapsed cuticles of the agricultural class throughout India.

When the idea of holding famines was first started, I proposed to illustrate the project by stopping the pay and allowances of the Government of India for a month. But this did not listen to my proposal. People seldom listen to my proposals; and sometimes I think that this accounts for my constitutional melancholy.

You will ask, "What has all this talk of food and famine to do with the villager?" I reply, "Everything." Famine is the horizon of the Indian villager; insufficient food is the foreground. And this is the more extraordinary since the villager is surrounded by a dreamland of plenty. Everywhere you see fields flooded deep with millet and wheat. The village and its old trees have to climb on to a knoll to keep their feet out of the glorious poppy and the luscious sugar-cane. Sumptuous cream-coloured bullocks move sleepily about with an air of luxurious sloth; and sleek Brahmans utter their lazy prayers while bathing languidly in the water and sunshine of the tank Even the buffaloes have nothing to do, but float the livelong day deeply immersed in the bulrushes. Everything is steeped in repose. The bees murmur their idylls among the flowers; the doves moan their amorous complaints from the shady leafage of pipal trees; out of the cool recesses of wells the idle cooing of the pigeons ascends into the summer-laden air; the rainbow-fed chameleon slumbers on the branch; the enamelled beetle on the leaf; the little fish in the sparkling depths below; the radiant kingfisher, tremulous as sunlight, in mid-air; and the peacock, with furled glories, on the temple tower of the silent gods. Amid this easeful and luscious splendour the villager labours and starves.

Reams of hiccoughing platitudes lodged in the pigeon-holes of the Home Office by all the gentlemen clerks and gentlemen farmers of the world cannot mend this. While the Indian villager has to maintain the glorious phantasmagoria of an imperial policy, while he has to support legions of scarlet soldiers, golden chuprassies, purple politicals, and green commissions, he must remain the hunger-stricken, over driven phantom he is.

While the eagle of Thought rides the tempest in scorn,
Who cares if the lightning is burning the corn?

If Old England is going to maintain her throne and her swagger in our vast Orient she ought to pay up like a—man, I was going to say; for, according to the old Sanscrit proverb, "You can get nothing for nothing, and deuced little for a halfpenny." These unpaid-for glories bring nothing but shame.

But even the poor Indian cultivator has his joys beneath the clouds of Revenue Boards and Famine Commissions. If we look closely at his life we may see a soft glory resting upon it. I am not Mr. Caird, and I do not intend entering into the technical details of agriculture—"*Quid de utilitate loquar stercorandi?*" —but I would say something of that sweetness which a close communion with earth and heaven must shed upon the silence of lonely labour in the fields. God is ever with the cultivator in all the manifold sights and sounds of this marvellous world of His. In that mysterious temple of the Dawn, in which we of noisy mess-rooms, heated courts, and dusty offices are infrequent worshippers, the peasant is a priest. There he offers up his hopes and fears for rain and sunshine; there he listens to the anthems of birds we rarely hear, and interprets auguries that for us have little meaning.

The beast of prey skulking back to his lair, the stag quenching his thirst ere retiring to the depths of the forest, the wedge of wild fowl flying with trumpet notes to some distant lake, the vulture hastening in heavy flight to the carrion that night has provided, the crane flapping to the shallows, and the jackal shuffling along to his shelter in the nullah, have each and all their portent to the initiated eye. Day, with its fierce glories, brings the throbbing silence of intense life, and under flickering shade, amid the soft pulsations of Nature, the cultivator lives his day-dream. What there is of squalor, and drudgery, and carking care in his life melts into a brief oblivion, and he is a man in the presence of his God with the holy stillness of Nature brooding over him. With lengthening shadows comes labour and a re-awaking. The air is once more full of all sweet sounds, from the fine whistle of the kite, sailing with supreme dominion through the azure depths of air, to the stir and buzzing chatter of little birds and crickets among the leaves and grass. The egret has resumed his fishing in the tank where the rain is stored for the poppy and sugar-cane fields, the sand-pipers bustle along the margin, or wheel in little silvery clouds over the bright waters, the gloomy cormorant sits alert on the stump of a dead date-tree, the busy black divers hurry in and out of the weeds, and ever and anon shoot under the water in hot quest of some tiny fish ; the whole machinery of life and death is in full play, and our villager shouts to his patient oxen and lives his life. Then gradual darkness, and food with homely joys, a little talk, a little tobacco, a few sad songs, and kindly sleep.

The villages are of immemorial antiquity; their names, their traditions, their hereditary offices have come down out of the dim past through countless generations. History sweeps over them with her trampling armies and her conquerors, her changing dynasties and her shifting laws—sweeps over them and leaves them unchanged.

The village is self-contained. It is a complete organism, protoplastic it may be, with the chlorophyll of age colouring its institutions, but none the less a perfect, living entity. It has within itself everything that its existence demands, and it has no ambition. The torment of frustrated hope and of supersession is unknown in the village. We who are always striving to roll our prospects and our office boxes up the hill to Simla may learn a lesson here :

Sisyphus in vita quoque nobis ante oculos est
Qui petere a populo fasces sævasque secures
Imbibit et semper victus tristisque recedit.
Nam petere imperium quod inanest nec datur umquam,
Atque in eo semper durum sufferre laborem,
Hoc est adverso nixantem trudere monte
Saxum quod tamen e summo jam vertice rusum
Volvitur et plani raptim petit æquora campi.

In this idyllic existence, in which, as I have said, there is no ambition, several other ills are also wanting. There is, for instance, no News in the village. The village is without the pale of intelligence. This must indeed be bliss. Just fancy, dear Vanity, a state of existence in which there are no politics, no discoveries, no travels, no speculations, no Garnet Wolseleys, no Gladstones, no Captain Careys, no Sarah Bernhardts! If there be a heaven upon earth, it is surely here. Here no Press Commissioner sits on the hillside croaking dreary translations from the St. Petersburg press; here no *Pioneer* sings catches with Sir John Strachey in Council. But here the lark sings in heaven for evermore, the sweet corn grows below, and the villager, amid the quiet joys with which earth fills her lap, dreams his low life.

No. XV.

THE OLD COLONEL.

No. XV.

THE OLD COLONEL.

" Kwaihaipeglaoandjeldikaro."—*Rigmarole Veda.*

THE old Indian Colonel ripening for pension on the shelf of General Duty is an object at once pitiful and ludicrous. His profession has ebbed away from him, and he lies a melancholy derelict on the shore, with sails flapping idly against the mast and meaningless pennants streaming in the wind.

He has forgotten nearly everything he ever learnt of military duty, and what he has not forgotten has been changed. It is as much as he can do to keep up with the most advanced thoughts of the Horse Guards on buttons and gold lace. Yet he is still employed sometimes to turn out a guard, or to swear that "the Service is going," &c.; and though he has lost his nerve for riding, he has still a good seat on a boot-lace committee.

He is a very methodical old man. He rises at an early hour, strolls down to the Club on the Mall—perhaps the Wheler Club, perhaps some other—has his tea, newspaper, and gossip there; and then back to his small bungalow. After breakfast he arrays himself for the day in some nondescript white uniform, and with a forage cap stuck gaily on one side of his head, a cheroot in his mouth, and a large white umbrella in his hand, he again sallies forth to the Club. An old horse is led behind him.

Now the serious business of life again begins—to get through the day. There are six newspapers to read, twelve pegs to drink, four-and-twenty Madras cheroots to smoke, there is kindly tiffin to linger over, forty winks afterwards, a game of billiards, the band on the Mall, dinner, and over all, incessant chatter, chatter, old scandal, old jokes, and old stories. Everyone likes the old Colonel, of course. Everyone says, "Here comes poor old Smith; what an infernal bore he is!"—"Hulloa, Colonel, how are you? glad to see you! what's the news? how's exchange?"

The old Colonel is not avaricious, but he saves money. He cannot help it. He has no tastes and he draws very large pay. His mind, therefore, broods over questions relating to the investment of money, the depreciation of silver, and the saving effected by purchasing things at co-operative stores. He never really solves any problem suggested by these topics. His mind is not prehensile like the tail of the Apollo Bundar; everything eludes its grasp; so its pursuits are interminable. The old Colonel's cerebral caloric burns with a feeble flicker, like that of the Madras secretariats. It never consumes a subject. The same theme is always fresh fuel. You might say the same thing to him every morning at the same hour till the crack of doom, and he would never recollect that he had heard your remark before. This certainly must give a freshness to life and render eternity possible.

The old Colonel is not naturally an indolent man, but the prominent fact about him is that he has nothing to do. If you gave him a sun-dial to take care of, or a rain-gauge to watch, or a secret to keep, he would be quite delighted. I once asked Smith to keep a secret of mine, and the poor old fellow was so much afraid of losing it that in a few hours he had got everybody in the station helping him to keep it. It always surprises me that men with so much time on their hands do not become Political Agents.

Sometimes our old Colonel gets into the flagitious habit of writing for the newspapers. He talks himself into thinking that he possesses a grievance, so he puts together a fasciculus of lop-sided sentences, gets the ideas set straight by the Doctor, the spelling refurbished by the Padré, and fires off the product to the *Pioneer*. Then days of feverish excitement supervene, hope alternating with tear. Will it appear? Will the Commander-in-Chief be offended? Will the Government of India be angry? What will the Service say?

The old Colonel is always rather suspicious of the great cocked-hats at head-quarters. He knows that to maintain an air of activity they must still be changing something, or abolishing something; and he is always afraid that they will change, or abolish him. But how could they change the old Colonel? In a regiment he would be like Alice in Wonderland; on the Staff he would be like old wine in a new bottle. They might make him a K.C.B., it is true; but he does not belong to the Simla Band of Hope, and stars must not be allowed to shoot madly from their sphere. As to abolishing the old Colonel, this too presents its difficulties, for Sir Norman Henry and all the celebrated cocked-hats at home and abroad look upon the Indian Staff Corps as Pygmalion looked on his Venus. They dote upon its lifeless charms, and (figuratively) love to clasp it in their foolish arms.

It is better to dress him up in an old red coat, and strap him on to an old sword with a brass scabbard, that he may stand up on high ceremonials and drink the health of the good Queen for whom he has lived bravely through sunshine and stormy weather, in defiance of epidemics, retiring schemes, and the Army Medical Department. It is good to ask him to place his old knees under your hospitable board, and to fill him with wholesome wine, while he decants the mellow stories of an Anglo-India that is speedily dissolving from view.

The old Colonel has no harm in him; his scandal blows upon the grandmothers of people that have passed away, and his little improprieties are such as might illustrate a sermon of the present day.

But you must never speak to him as if his sun were setting. He is as hopeful as a two-year-old. Every Gazette thrills him with vague expectations and alarms. If he found himself in orders for a Brigade he would be less surprised than anyone in the Army. He never ceases to hope that something may turn up—that something tangible may issue from the circumambient world of conjecture. But nothing will ever turn up for our poor old Colonel till his poor old toes turn up to the daisies. This change only, which we harshly call "Death," will steal over his prospects; this new slide only will be slipped into the magic lantern of his existence, accompanied by funeral drums and slow marching.

Soon we shall hardly be able to decipher his name and age on the crumbling gravestone among the weeds of our horrible station cemetery—but what matters it?

"For his bones are dust,
And his sword is rust,
And his soul is with the saints, we trust."

No. XVI.

THE CIVIL SURGEON.

No. XVI.

THE CIVIL SURGEON.

"Throw physic to the dogs, I'll none of it."

PERHAPS you would hardly guess from his appearance and ways that he was a surgeon and a medicine-man. He certainly does not smell of lavender or peppermint, or display fine and curious linen, or tread softly like a cat. Contrariwise.

He smells of tobacco, and wears flannel underclothing. His step is heavy. He is a gross, big, cow-buffalo sort of man, with a tangled growth of beard. His ranting voice and loud familiar manner amount to an outrage. He laughs like a camel, with deep bubbling noises. Thick corduroy breeches and gaiters swaddle his shapeless legs, and he rides a coarse-bred Waler mare.

I pray the gods that he may never be required to operate upon my eyes, or intestines, or any other delicate organ—that he may never be required to trephine my skull, or remove the roof of my mouth.

Of course he is a very good fellow. He walks straight into your drawing-room with a pipe in his mouth, bellowing out your name. No servant announces his arrival. He tramples in and crushes himself into a chair, without removing his hat, or performing any other high ceremonial. He has been riding in the sun, and is in a state of profuse perspiration; you will have to bring him round with the national beverage of Anglo-India, a brandy-and-soda.

Now he will enter upon your case. "Well, you're looking very blooming; what the devil is the matter with you? Eh? Eh? Want a trip to the hills? Eh? Eh? How is the bay pony? Eh? Have you seen Smith's new filly? Eh?"

This is very cheerful and reassuring if you are a healthy man with some large conspicuous disease—a broken rib, cholera, or toothache; but if you are a fine, delicately-made man, pregnant with poetry as the egg of the nightingale is pregnant with music, and throbbing with an exquisite nervous sensibility, perhaps languishing under some vague and occult disease, of which you are only conscious in moments of intense introspection, this mode of approaching the diagnosis is apt to give your system a shock.

Otherwise it may be bracing, like the inclement north wind. But, speaking for myself, it has proved most ruinous and disastrous. Since I have known the Doctor my constitution has broken up. I am a wreck. There is hardly a single drug in the whole pharmacopœia that I can now take with any pleasure, and I have entirely lost sight of a most interesting and curious complaint.

You see, dear Vanity, that I don't mince

matters. I take our Doctor as I find him, rough and allopathic; but I am sure he might be improved in course of two or three generations. We may leave this, however, to Nature and the Army Medical Department. Reform is not my business. I have no proposals to offer that will accelerate the progress of the Doctor towards a higher type.

Happily his surgical and medicinal functions claim only a portion of his time. He is in charge of the district gaol, a large and comfortable retreat for criminals. Here he is admirable. To some eight or nine hundred murderers, robbers, and inferior delinquents he plays the part of *maître d'hôtel* with infinite success. In the whole country side you will not find a community so well bathed, dressed, exercised, fed, and lodged as that over which the Doctor presides. You observe on every face a quiet Quakerish air of contentment. Every inmate of the gaol seems to think that he has now found a haven of rest.

If the sea-horse on the ocean
  Own no dear domestic cave,
Yet he slumbers without motion
  On the still and halcyon wave:

If on rainy days the loafer
  Gamble when he cannot roam,
The police will help him so far
  As to find him here a home.

This is indeed a quiet refuge for world-wearied men; a sanctuary undisturbed by the fears of the weak or the passions of the strong. All reasonable wants are gratified here; nothing is hoped for any more. The poor burglar burdened with unsaleable "grab" and the reproaches of a venal world sorrowfully seeks an asylum here. He brings nothing in his hand; he seeks nothing but rest. He whispers through the key-hole—

"Nil cupientium
Nudus castra peto."

Look at this prisoner slumbering peacefully beside his *huqqa* under the suggestive bottle tree (there is something touching in his selecting the shade of a *bottle* tree: Horace clearly had no *bottle* tree; or he would never have lain under a strawberry (and cream) tree). You can see that he has been softly nurtured. What a sleek, sturdy fellow he is! He is a covenanted servant here, having passed an examination in gang robbery accompanied by violence and prevarication. He cannot be discharged under a long term of years. Uncovenanted pilferers, in for a week, regard him with respect and envy. And certainly his lot is enviable: he has no cares, no anxieties. Famine and the depreciation of silver are nothing to him. Rain or sunshine, he lives in plenty. His days are spent in an innocent round of duties, relieved by sleep and contemplation of τὸ ὄν. In the long heats of summer he whiles away the time with carpet-making; between the showers of autumn he digs, like our first parents, in the Doctor's garden; and in winter, as there is no billiard-table, he takes a turn on the treadmill with his mates. Perhaps, as he does so, he recites Charles Lamb's Pindaric ode :—

"Great mill!
That by thy motion proper
(No thanks to wind or sail, or toiling rill)
Grinding that stubborn corn, the human will,
Turn'st out men's consciences,
Than were begrimed before, as clean and sweet
As flour from purest wheat,
Into thy hopper."

Yet sometimes a murmur rises like a summer zephyr even from the soft lap of luxury and ease. Even the hardened criminal, dandled on the knee of a patriarchal Government, will sometimes complain and try to give the Doctor trouble. But the Doctor has a specific—a brief incantation that allays every species of inflammatory discontent. "Look here, my man! If I hear any more of this infernal nonsense, I'll turn you out of the gaol neck and crop." This is a threat that never fails to produce the desired effect. To be expelled from gaol and driven, like Cain, into the rude and wicked world, a wanderer, an outcast—this would indeed be a cruel ban. Before such a presentiment the well-ordered mind of the criminal recoils with horror.

The Civil Surgeon is also a rain doctor, and takes charge of the Imperial gauge. If a pint more or a pint less than usual falls, he at once telegraphs this priceless gossip to the Press Commissioner, Oracle Grotto, Delphi, Elysium. This is one of our precautions to guard against famine. Mr. Caird is the other.

No. XVII.

THE SHIKARRY.

No. XVII.

THE SHIKARRY.

I HAVE come out to spend a day in the jungle with him, to see him play on his own stage. His little flock of white tents have flown many a march to meet me, and have now alighted at this accessible spot near a poor hamlet on the verge of cultivation. I feel that I have only to yield myself for a few days to their hospitable importunities and they will waft me away to profound forest depths, to the awful penetralia of the bison and the tiger. Even here everything is strange to me; the common native has become a Bheel, the sparrowhawk an eagle, the grass of the field a vast, reedy growth in which an elephant becomes a mere field-mouse. Out of the leaves come strange bird-notes, a strange silence broods over us; it is broken by strange rustlings and cries; it closes over us again strangely. Nature swoons in its glory of sunshine and weird music; it has put forth its powers in colossal timber and howling beasts of prey; it faints amid little wild flowers, fanned by breezes and butterflies.

My heart beats in strange anapæsts. This dream-world of leaf and bird stirs the blood with a strange enchantment. The Spirit of Nature touches us with her caduceus:—

> "Fair are others, none behold thee;
> But thy voice sounds low and tender
> Like the fairest, for it folds thee
> From the sight, that liquid splendour;
> And all feel, yet see thee never,
> As I feel now . . . ."

Our tents are played upon by the flickering shadows of the vast pipal-tree that rises in a laocoön turtuosity of roots out of an old well. The spot is cool and pleasant. Round us are picketed elephants, camels, bullocks, and horses, all enjoying the shade. Our servants are cooking their food on the precincts; each is busy in front of his own little mud fire-place. On a larger altar greater sacrifices are being offered up for our breakfast. A crowd of nearly naked Bheels watch the rites and snuff the fragrant incense of venison from a respectful distance. Their leader, a broken-looking old man, with hardly a rag on, stands apart exchanging deep confidences with my friend the Shikarry. This old Bheel is girt about the loins with knives, pouches, powder-horns, and ramrods; and he carries on his shoulder an aged flintlock. He looks old enough to be an English General Officer or a Cabinet Minister; and you might assume that he was in the last stage of physical and mental decay. But you would be quite wrong. This old Bheel will sit up all night on the branch of a tree among the horned owls; he will see the tiger kill the young buffalo tied up as a bait beneath; he will see it drink the life-blood and tear the haunch; he will watch it steal away and hide under the *karaunda* bush;

he will sit there till day breaks, when he will creep under the thorn jungle, across the stream, up the scarp of the ravine, through the long grass to the sahib's camp, and give the word that makes the hunter's heart dance. From the camp he will stride from hamlet to hamlet till he has raised an army of beaters; and he will be back at the camp with his forces before the sahib has breakfasted. Through the long heats of the day he will be the life and soul of the hunt, urging on the beaters with voice and example, climbing trees, peeping under bushes, carrying orders, giving advice, changing the line, until that supreme moment when shots are fired, when the rasping growl tells that the shots have taken effect, and when at length the huge striped cat lies stretched out dead. And all this on a handful of parched grain!

My friend the Shikarry delights to clothe himself in the coarse fabrics manufactured in gaols, which, when properly patched and decorated with pockets, have undoubtedly a certain wild-wood appearance. As the hunter does not happen to be a Bheel with the privileges of nakedness conferred by a brown skin, this is perhaps the only practical alternative. If he went out to shoot in evening clothes, a crush hat, and a hansom cab, the chances are that he would make an example of himself and come to some untimely end. What would the Apollo Bundar say? What would the Bengali Baboo say? What would the sea-aye-ees says? Yes, our hunter affects coarse and snuffy clothes; they carry with them suggestions of hardship and roughing it; and his hat is umbrageous and old.

As to the man under the hat, he is an odd compound of vanity, sentiment, and generosity. He is as affected as a girl. Among other traits he affects reticence, and he will not tell me what the plans for the day are, or what *khabbar* has been received. Knowing absolutely nothing, he moves about with a solemn and important air, and he says to me, "Don't fret yourself, my dear fellow; you'll know all about it, time enough. I have made arrangements." Then he dissembles and talks of irrelevant topics transcendentally. This makes me feel such a poor pen-and-ink fellow, such a worm, such a political agent!

With this discordant note still vibrating we go in to breakfast; and then, dear Vanity, he bucks with a quiet, stubborn determination that would fill an American editor or an Under-Secretary of State with despair. He belongs to the twelve-foot-tiger school; so, perhaps, he can't help it.

If the whole truth were told, he is a warm-hearted, generous, plucky fellow, with boundless vanity and a romantic vein of maudlin sentiment that seduces him from time to time into the gin-and-water corner of an Indian newspaper. Under the heading of "The Forest Ranger's Lament," or "The Old Shikarry's Tale of Woe," he hiccoughs his column of sickly lines (with St. Vitus's dance in their feet), and then I believe he feels better. I have seen him do it; I have caught him in criminal conversation with a pen and a sheet of paper; a bottle at hand—

> A quo, ceu fonte perenni,
> Vatum Pieriis ora rigantur aquis.

In appearance he is a very short man with

a long black beard, a sunburnt face, and a clay pipe. He has shot battalions of tigers and speared squadrons of wild pig. He is universally loved, universally admired, and universally laughed at.

He is generous to a fault. All the young fellows for miles round owe him money. He would think there was something wrong if they did not borrow from him; and yet, somehow, I don't think that he is very well off. There is nothing in his bungalow but guns, spears, and hunting trophies; he never goes home, and I have an idea that there is some heavy drain on his purse in the whole country. But you should hear him troll a hunting song with his grand organ voice, and you would fancy him the richest man in the world, his note is so high and triumphant!

So when in after days we boast
  Of many wild boars slain,
We'll not forget our runs to toast
  Or run them o'er again.

And when our memory's mirror true
  Reflects the scenes of yore,
We'll think of *him* it brings to view,
  Who loved to hunt the boar.

No. XVIII.

THE GRASS-WIDOW IN NEPHELOCOCCYGIA.

"Her bosom's lord sits lightly on his throne?"

LITTLE Mrs. Lollipop has certainly proved a source of disappointment to her lady friends. They have watched her for three seasons going lightly and merrily through all the gaieties of Cloudland; they have listened to the scandal of the cuckoos among the pine-trees and rhododendrons, but they have not caught her tripping. Oh, no, they will never catch her tripping. She does not trip for their amusement: perhaps she trips it when they go on the light fantastic toe, but there is no evidence; there is only a zephyr of conjecture, only the world's low whisper not yet broken into storm —not yet.

Yes, she is a source of disappointment to them. They have noted her points; her beauty has burned itself into their jealousy; her merry laugh has fanned their scorn; her bountiful presence is an affront to them, as is her ripe and lissom figure. They pronounce her morally unsound; they say her nature has a taint; they chill her popularity with silent smiles of slow disparagement. But they have no particulars; their slander is not concrete. It is an amorphous accusation, sweeping and vague, spleen-born and proofless.

She certainly knows how to dress. Her weeds sit easily and smoothly on their delightful mould. You might think of her as a sweet, warm statue painted in water-colours. (Who wouldn't be her Pygmalion?) If she adds a garment it is an improvement; if she removes a garment it is an improvement; if she dresses her hair it is better; if she lets it

No. XVIII.

THE GRASS-WIDOW IN NEPHELOCOCCYGIA.

fall in a brown cascade over her white shoulders it is still better; when it is yet in curl-papers it is charming. If you smudge the tip of her nose with a burnt cork the effect is irresistible; if you stick a flower in her hair it is a fancy dress, a complete costume—she becomes Flora, Aurora, anything you like to name. Yet I have never clothed her in a flower, I have never smudged her nose with a burnt cork, I have never uncurled her hair. Ali Baba's character must not go drifting down the stream of gossip with the Hill Captains and the Under-Secretaries. But I hope that this does not destroy the argument. The argument is that she is quite too delightful, and therefore blown upon by poisonous whispers.

Her bungalow is on Elysium, of course; it is a cottage with a verandah, built on a steep slope, and buried deep in shrubbery and trees. Within all is plain, but exquisitively neat. A wood fire is burning gaily, and the kindly tea-tray is at hand. It is five o'clock. Clean servants move silently about with hot water, cake, &c. The little boy, a hostage from papa in the warm plains below, is sitting pensive, after the fashion of Anglo-Indian children, in a little chair. His bearer crouches behind him. The unspeakable widow, in a tea-gown dimly splendid with tropical végetation in neutral tints, holds a piece of chocolate in her hand, while she leans back in her fauteuil convulsed with laughter. (It is not necessary to say that Ali Baba is relating one of his improving tales.) How pretty she looks, showing her excellent teeth and suffused with bright warm blushes. As I gaze upon her with fond amazement, I murmur mechanically :—

> Mine be a cot beside the hill;
>   A tea-pot's hum shall soothe my ear,
> A widowy girl, that likes me still,
>   With many a smile shall linger near.

I have been asked to write a philosophical minute on the mental and moral condition of delightful Mrs. Lollipop's husband who lives down in the plains. I have been requested by the Press Commissioner to inquire in Government fashion, with pen and ink, as to whether the complaisant proprietor of so many charms desires to have a recheat winded in his forehead, and to hang his bugle in an invisible baldrick; whether it is true in his case that Love's ear will hear the lowest cuckoo note, and that Love's perception of gossip is more soft and sensible than are the tender horns of cockled snails. Towards all these points I have directed my researches. I have resolved myself into a Special Commission, and I have sat upon grass-widowers *in camera*. If I sit a little longer a Report will be hatched, which, of course, I shall take to England, and when there I shall go to the places of amusement with the Famine Commission, and have rather a good time of it. Already I can see, with that bright internal eye which requires no lime-light, grim Famine stalking about the Aquarium after dinner with a merry jest preeing its wings on his lips.

But what has all this talk of country matters to do with little Mrs. Lollipop? Absolutely nothing. She thinks no ill of herself. She is the most charitable woman in the world. There is no veil of sin over her eye; no cloud of suspicion darkens her forehead; no concealment feeds upon her damask cheek. Like

Eve she goes about hand in hand with her friends, in native innocence, relying on what she has of virtue. Sweet simplicity! sweet confidence! My eagle quill shall not flutter these doves.

Have you ever watched her at a big dance? She takes possession of some large warrior who has lately arrived fram the battle-fields of Umballa or Meerut, and she chaperones him about the rooms, staying him with flagons and prattling low nothings. The weaker vessel jibs a little at first; but gradually the spell begins to work and the love-light kindles in his eye. He dances, he makes a joke, he tells a story, he turns round and looks her in the face. He is lost. That big centurion is a casualty; and no one pities him. "How can he go on like that, odious creature!" say the withered wall-flowers, and the Hill Captains fume round, working out formulæ to express his baseness But he is away on the glorious mountains of vanity; the intoxicating atmosphere makes life tingle in his blood; he is an ἀεροβάτης, he no longer treads the earth. In a few days Mrs. Lollipop will receive a post-

card from the Colonel of her centurion's regiment.

"MY DEAR MRS.

Lollipop, dic, per omnes
Te deos oro, Robinson cur properes amando
Perdere? cur apricum
Oderit campum, patiens pulveris atque solis.
Yrs. Sincy.
HORACE FITZDOTTREL."

Ten to one an Archdeacon will be sent for to translate this. Ten to one there is a shindy, ending in tea and tearful smiles; for she is bound to get a blowing up.

After what I have written I suppose it would be superfluous to affirm with oaths my irrefragable belief in Mrs. Lollipop's innocence; it would be superfluous to deprecate the many-winged slanders that wound this milk-white hind. If, however, by swearing, any of your readers think I can be of service to her character, I hope they will let me know. I have learnt a few oaths lately that I reckon will unsphere some of the scandal-mongers of Nephelococcygia. I had my ear one morning at the key-hole when the Army Commission was revising the cursing and swearing code for field service.—(Ah! these dear old Generals, what depths of simplicity they disclose when they get by themselves. I sometimes think that if I had my life to live over again I would keep a newspaper and become a really great General. I know some five or six obscure aboriginal tribes that have never yet yielded a single war or a single K.C.B.)

But this is a digression. I was maintaining the goodness of Mrs. Lollipop—little Mrs. Lollipop! sweet little Mrs. Lollipop! I was going to say that she was far too good to be made the subject of whisperings and inuendoes Her virtue is of such a robust type that even a Divorce Court would sink back abashed before it, like a guilty thing surprised. Indeed, she often reminds me of Cæsar's wife.

The harpies of scandal protest that she dresses too low; that she exposes too freely the well-rounded charms of her black silk stockings; that she appears at fancy-dress balls picturesquely unclothed—in a word, that the public see a little too much of little Mrs. Lollipop; and that, in conversation with men, she nibbles at the forbidden apples of thought.

But all this proves her innocence, surely. She fears no danger, for she knows no sin. She cannot understand why she should hide anything from an admiring world. Why keep her charms concealed from mortal eye, like roses that in deserts bloom and die? She often reminds me of Una in Hypocrisy's cell.

I heard an old Gorgon ask one of Mrs. Lollipop's *clientèle* the other day whether he would like to be Mrs. Lollipop's husband. "No," he said, "not her husband; I am not worthy to be the husband—

"But I would be the necklace,
And all day long to fall and rise
Upon her balmy bosom
With her laughter or her sighs;
And I would lie so light, so light,
I scarce should be unclasped at night."

That old Gorgon is now going through a course of hysterics under medical and clerical advice. Her ears are in as bad a case as Lady Macbeth's hands. Hymns will not purge them.

No. XIX.

THE TRAVELLING M.P.

THE BRITISH LION RAMPANT.

No. XIX.

THE TRAVELLING M.P.

THE BRITISH LION RAMPANT.

There is not a more fearful wild fowl than your travelling M.P. This unhappy creature, whose mind is a perfect blank regarding *Faujdari* and *Bandobast*, and who cannot distinguish the molluscous baboo from the osseous pathan, will actually presume to discuss Indian subjects with you, unless strict precautions be taken.

When I meet one of these loose M.P.'s

ramping about I always cut his claws at once. I say, "Now, Mr. T. G., you must understand that according to my standard you are a homunculus of the lowest type. There is nothing I value a man for that you can do; there is nothing I consider worth directing the human mind upon that you know. If you ask for any information which I may deem it expedient to give to a person in your unfortunate position, well and good; but if you venture to argue with me, to express any opinion, to criticise anything I may be good enough to say regarding India, or to quote any passage relating to Asia from the works of Burke, Cowper, Bright, or Fawcett, I will hand you over to Major Henderson for strangulation, I will cause your body to be burnt by an Imperial Commission of sweepers, and I will mention your name in the *Pioneer*."

In dangerous cases, where a note-book is carried, your loose M.P. must be made to reside within the pale of guarded conversation. If you are wise you will speak to him in the interrogative mood exclusively; and you will treat his answers with contumelious laughter or disdainful silence.

About a week after your M.P. has landed in India he will begin his great work on the history, literature, philosophy, and social institutions of the Hindoos. You will see him in a railway carriage when stirred by the οἶστρος studying Forbes's Hindustani Manual. He is undoubtedly writing the chapter on the philology of the Aryan Family. Do you observe the fine frenzy that kindles behind his spectacles as he leans back and tries to eject a root? These pangs are worth about half-a-crown an hour in the present state of the book market. One cannot contemplate them without profound emotion.

The reading world is hunger-bitten about Asia, and I often think I shall take three months' leave and run up a *précis* of Sanskrit and Pali literature, just a few folios for the learned world. Max Müller begs me to learn these languages first; but this would be a toil and drudgery, whereas to me the pursuit of literary excellence and fame is a mere amusement, like lawn-tennis or rinking. It is the fault of the age to make a labour of what is meant to be a pastime.

> "Telle est de nos plaisirs la surface légère;
> Glissez, mortels, n'appuyez pas."

The travelling M.P. will probably come to you with a letter of introduction from the last station he has visited, and he will immediately proceed to make himself quite at home in your bungalow with the easy manners of the Briton abroad. He will acquaint you with his plans and name the places of interest in the neighbourhood which he requires you to show him. He will ask you to take him, as a preliminary canter, to the gaol and lunatic asylum; and he will make many interesting suggestions to the civil surgeon as to the management of these institutions, comparing them unfavourably with those he has visited in other stations. He will then inspect the Brigadier-General commanding the station, the chaplain, and the missionaries. On his return—when he ought to be bathing—he will probably write his article for the *Twentieth*

Century, entitled "Is India Worth Keeping?" And this ridiculous old Shrovetide cock, whose ignorance and information leave two broad streaks of laughter in his wake, is turned loose upon the reading public! Upon my word I believe the reading public would do better to go and sit at the feet of Baboo Sillabub Thunder Gosht, B.A.

What is it that these travelling people put on paper? Let me put it in the form of a conundrum. *Q*. What is it that the travelling M.P. treasures up and the Anglo-Indian hastens to throw away? *A*. Erroneous, hazy, distorted first impressions

Before the eyes of the griffin, India steams up in poetical mists, illusive, fantastic, subjective, ideal, picturesque. The adult *Qui Hai* attains to prose, to stern and disappointing realities; he removes the gilt from the Empire and penetrates to the brown ginger-bread of Rajas and Baboos. One of the most serious duties attending a residence in India is the correcting of those misapprehensions which your travelling M.P. sacrifices his bath to hustle upon paper. The spectacled people embalmed in secretariats alone among Anglo-Indians continued to see the gay visions of griffinhood. They alone preserve the phantasmagoria of bookland and dreamland. As for the rest of us:—

> Out of the day and night
> A joy has taken flight:
> Baboos and Rajas and Indian lore
> Moved our faint hearts with grief, but with delight
> No more—oh, never more!

It is strange that one who is modest and inoffensive in his own country should immediately on leaving it exhibit some of the worst features of 'Arrỳism; but it seems inevitable. I have met in this unhappy land, countrymen (who are gentlemen in England, Members of Parliament, and Deputy-Lieutenants, and that kind of thing) whose conduct and demeanour while here I can never recall without tears and blushes for our common humanity. My friends witnessing this emotion often suppose that I am thinking of the Famine Commission.

As far as I can learn, it is a generally received opinion at home that a man who has seen the Taj at Agra, the Qutb at Delhi, and the Duke at Madras, has graduated with honours in all questions connected with British interests in Asia; and is only unfitted for the office of Governor-General of India from knowing too much.

No. XX.

MEM-SAHIB.

No. XX.

MEM-SAHIB.

" Her life is lone. He sits apart ;
He loves her yet : she will not weep,
Tho' rapt in matters dark and deep
He seems to slight her simple heart.

For him she plays, to him she sings
Of early faith and plighted vows ;
She knows but matters of the house,
And he, he knows a thousand things."

I FIRST met her shepherding her little flock across the ocean. She was a beautiful woman, in the full sweetness and bloom of life. Her talk was of the busy husband she had left, the station life, the attached servants, the favourite horse, the garden and the bungalow. Her husband would soon follow her, in a year, or two years, and they would return together; but they would return to a silent home—the children would be left behind She was going home to her mother and sisters; but there had been changes in this home. So her thoughts were woven of hopes and fears; and, as she sat on deck of an evening, with the great heart of the moon-lit sea palpitating around us, and the homeless night-wind sighing through the cordage, she would sing to us one of the plaintive ballads of the old country, till we forgot to listen to the sobbing and the trampling of the engines, and till all sights and sounds resolved themselves into a temple of sentiment round a charming priestess chanting low anthems. She would leave us early to go to her babies. She would leave us throbbing with mock heroics, undecided whether we should cry, or consecrate our lives to some high and noble enterprise, or drink one more glass of hot whiskey-and-water. She was kind, but not sentimental; her sweet, yet practical "good-ental" was quite of the work-a-day world; we felt that it tended to dispel illusions.

She had three little boys, who were turned out three times a-day in the ultimate state of good behaviour, tidiness, and cleanliness, and who lapsed three times a-day into a state of original sin combined with tar and ship's grease. These three little boys pervaded the vessel with an innocent smile on their three little faces, their mother's winning smile. Every man on the ship was their own familiar friend, bound to them by little interchanges of biscuits, confidences, twine, and by that electric smile which their mother communicated, and from which no one wished to be insulated. Yes, they quite pervaded the vessel, these three little innocents, flying that bright and friendly smile; and there was no description of mischief suitable for three very little boys that they did not exhaust. The ingenuity they squandered every day in doing a hundred things which they ought not to have done was perfectly marvellous. Before the voyage was half over we thought there was nothing left for them to do; but we were entirely mistaken. The daily round, a common cask would furnish all they had to ask; to them the meanest whistle that blows, or a pocket-knife, could give thoughts that too often led to smiles and tears.

Their mother's thoughts were ever with them; but she was like a hen with a brood of ducklings. They passed out of her element, and only returned as hunger called them. When they did return she was all that soap and water, loving reproaches, and tender appeals could be; and as they were very affectionate little boys, they were for the time thoroughly cleansed morally and physically, and sealed with the absolution of kisses.

I saw her three years afterwards in England. She was living in lodgings near a school which her boys attended. She looked careworn. Her relations had been kind to her, but not warmly affectionate. She had been disappointed with the welcome they had given her. They seemed changed to her, more formal, narrower, colder. She longed to be back in India; to be with her husband once more. But he was engrossed with his work. He wrote short letters enclosing cheques; but he never said that he missed her, that he longed to see her again, that she must come out to him, or that he must go to her. He could not have grown cold too? No, he was busy; he had never been demonstrative in his affection; this was his way. And she was anxious about the boys. She did not know whether they were really getting on, whether she was doing the best for them, whether their father would be satisfied. She had no friends near her, no one to speak to; so she brooded over these problems, exaggerated them, and fretted.

The husband was a man who lived in his own thoughts, and his thoughts were book thoughts. The world of leaf and bird, the circumambient firmament of music and light, shone in upon him through books. A book was the master-key that unlocked all his senses, that unfolded the varied landscape, animated the hero, painted the flower, swelled the orchestra of wind and ocean, peopled the plains of India with starvelings and the mountains of Afghanistan with cut-throats. Without a book he moved about like a shadow lost in some dim dreamland of echoes.

Everyone knew he was a scholar, and his thoughts had once or twice rung out to the world clear and loud as a trumpet-note through the oracles of the Press. But in society he was shy, awkward, and uncouth of speech, quite unable to marshal his thoughts, deserted by his memory, abashed before his own silences, and startled by his own words. Any fool who could talk about the legs of a horse or the height of a thermometer was Prospero to this social Caliban.

He felt that before the fine instincts of women his infirmity was especially conspicuous, and he drifted into misogyny, through bashfulness and pride; and yet misogyny was incompatible with his scheme of life and his ambition. He felt himself to be worthy of the full diapason of home life; he desired to be as other men were, besides being something more—

Κακὸν γυναῖχες' ἀλλ' ὅμως, ὦ δημόται,
Οὐκ ἐστὶγ δικειν οικιαν ἄνευ κακοῦ.
Καί γὰρ τὸ γῆμαι, καὶ τὸ μὴ γῆμαι, κακόν.

So he married her who loved him for choosing her, and who reverenced him for his mysterious treasures of thought.

There was much in his life that she could never share; but he longed for companionship in thought, and for the first year of their married life he tried to introduce her to his world. He led her slowly up to the quiet hill-tops of thought where the air is still and clear, and he gave her to drink of the magic fountains of music. Their hearts beat one delicious measure. Her gentle nature was plastic under the poet's touch, wrought in an instant to perfect harmony with love, or tears, or laughter. To read aloud to her in the evening after the day's work was over, and to see her stirred by every breath of the thought-storm, was to enjoy an exquisite interpretation of the poet's motive, like an impression bold and sharp from the matrix of the poet's mind. This was to hear the song of the poet and Nature's low echo. How tranquillising it was! How it effaced the petty vexations of the day!—"softening and concealing; and busy with a hand of healing."

Tale tuum carmen nobis, divine poeta,
Quale sopor fessis in gramine, quale per æstum
Dulcis aquæ saliente sitim restinguere rivo.

But with the advent of babies and after long separations poetry declined, and the sympathetic wife became more and more motherly. The father retired sadly into the cloudland of books. He will not emerge again. Husband and wife will stand upon the clear hill-tops together no more.

Neither quite knows what has happened; they both feel changed with an undefined sorrow, with a regret that pride will not enunciate. She is now again in India with her husband. There are duties, courtesies, nay, kindnesses which both will perform, but the ghost of love and sympathy will only rise in their hearts to gibber in mockery words and phrases that have lost their meaning, that have lost their enchantment.

"O Love! who bewailest
The frailty of all things here,
Why choose you the frailest
For your cradle, your home, and your bier?

Its passions will rock thee
  As the storms rock the raven on high;
Bright reason will mock thee
  Like the sun from a wintry sky.

From thy nest every rafter
  Will rot, and thine eagle home
Leave thee naked to laughter
  When leaves fall and cold winds come."

No. XXI.

ALI BABA ALONE;

THE LAST DAY.

No. XXI.

ALI BABA ALONE;

THE LAST DAY.

"Now the last of many days,
All beautiful and bright as thou,
The loveliest and the last is dead.
Rise, memory, and write its praise."

How shall I lay this spectre of my own identity? Shall I leave it to melt away gracefully in the light of setting suns? It would never do to put it out like a farthing rushlight after it had haunted the Great Ornamental in an aurora of smiles. Is Ali Baba to cease upon the midnight without pain? or is he to lie down like a tired child and weep out the spark? or should he just flit to Elysium? There, seated on Elysian lawns, browsed by none but Dian's (no allusion to little Mrs. Lollipop) fawns, amid the noise of fountains wonderous and the parle of voices thunderous, some wag might scribble on his door, "Here lies Ali Baba," as if glancing at his truthfulness. How is he to pass effectively into the golden silences? How is he to relapse into the still-world of observation? Would four thousand five hundred a month and Simla do it, with nothing to do and allowances, and a seat beside those littered under the swart Dog-Star of India? Or is it to be the mandragora of pension, that he may sleep out the great gap of *ennui* between this life and something better? How lonely the Government of India would feel! How the world would forget the Government of India! Voices would ask:—

"Do ye sit there still in slumber
In gigantic Alpine rows?
The black poppies out of number
Nodding, dripping from your brows
To the red lees of your wine—
And so kept alive and fine.

Sometimes I think that Ali Baba should be satisfied with the oblivion-mantle of knighthood and relapse into dingy respectability in the Avilion of Brompton or Bath; but since he has taken to wearing stars the accompanying itch for blood and fame has come:—

How doth the greedy K.C.B.
  Delight to brag and fight,
And gather medals all the day
  And wear them all the night.

The fear of being out-medalled and out-starred stings him.

Thus the desire to go hustling up the hill to the Temple of Fame with the other starry hosts impels him forward. If you mix yourself up with K.C.B.'s and raise your platform of ambition, you are just where you were at the A B C of your career. Living on a table-land, you experience no sensation of height. For the intoxicating delight of elevation you require a solitary pinnacle, some lonely eminence. Aut Cæsar, aut nullus; whether in the zenith or the nadir of the world's favour.

But how much more comfortable in the cold season than the chill splendours of the pinnacles of fame, where "pale suns unfelt at distance roll away," is a comfortable bungalow on the plains, with a little mulled claret after dinner. Here I think Ali Baba will be found, hidden from his creditors, the reading world, in the warm light of thought, singing songs unbidden till a few select cronies are wrought to sympathy with hopes and fears they heeded not—before the mulled claret.

To this symposium the A.-D.-C.-in-Waiting has invited himself on behalf of the Empire. He will sing the Imperial Anthem composed by Mr. Eastwick, and it will be translated into archaic Persian by an imperial Munshi for the benefit of the Man in Buckram, who will be present. The Man in Buckram, who is suffering from a cold in his heart, will be wrapped up in himself and a cocked hat. The Press Commissioner has also asked for an invitation. He will deliver a sentiment:—"Quid sit futuram cras fuge quærere." A Commander-in-Chief will tell the old story about the Service going to the dogs; after which there will be an interval of ten minutes allowed for swearing and hiccuping. The

Travelling M.P. will take the opportunity to jot down a few hasty notes on Aryan characteristics for the *Twentieth Century* before being placed under the table. The Baboo will subsequently be told off to sit on the Member's head. During this function the Baboo will deliver some sesquipedalian reflections in the rodomontade mood. The Shikarry will then dawdle over a twelve-foot-tiger story, while Mrs. Lollipop tells a fib and makes tea; and Ali Baba (unless his heart be too full of mulled claret) will make a joke. The company will break up at this point, after receiving a plenary dispensation from the Archdeacon.

Under such influences Ali Baba may become serious; he may learn from the wisdom of age and be cheered by the sallies of youth. But little Mrs. Lollipop can hardly be called one of the Sallies of his youth. Sally Lollipop rose upon the horizon of his middle age. She boiled up, pure blanc-mange and roses, over the dark brim of life's afternoon, a blushing sunrise, though late in dawning, and most cheerful. Sometimes after spending an afternoon with her, Ali Baba feels so cheered that the Government of India seems quite innocent and bright, like an old ballerina seen through the mists of champagne and lime light. He walks down the Mall smiling upon foolish Under-Secretaries and fat Baboos. The people whisper as he passes, "There goes Ali Baba"; and echo answers "Who is Ali Baba?" Then a little wind of conjecture breathes through the pine-trees and names are heard.

It is better not to call Ali Baba names. Nothing is so misleading as a vulgar nomenclature. I once knew a man who was called "Counsellor of the Empress" when he ought to have had his photograph exposed in the London shop-windows like King Cetewayo, K.C.M.G. I have heard an eminent Frontier General called "Judas Iscariot," and I myself was once pointed out as a "Famine Commissioner," and afterwards as an expurgated edition of the Secretary to the Punjab Government. People seemed to think that Ali Baba would smell sweeter under some other name. This was a mistake.

Almost everything you are told in Simla is a mistake. You should never believe anything you hear till it is contradicted by the *Pioneer*. I suppose the Government of India is the greatest *gobemouche* in the world. I suppose there never was an administration of equal importance which received so much information and which was so ill-informed. At a bureaucratic Simla dinner-party the abysses of ignorance that yawn below the company on every Indian topic are quite appalling!

I once heard Mr. Stokes say that he had never heard of my book on the Permanent Settlement; and yet Mr. Stokes is a decidedly intelligent man, with some knowledge of Cymric and law. I daresay now if you were to draw off and decant the law on his brain, it would amount to a full dose for an adult; yet he never heard of my book on the Permanent Settlement. He knew about Blackstone; he had seen an old copy once in a second-hand book shop; but he had never heard of my work! How loosely the world floats around us! I question its objective reality. I doubt whether anything has more objectivity in it than Ali Baba himself. He was certainly flogged at school. Yet when we now try to put our finger on Ali Baba he eludes the touch; when we try to lay him he starts up gibbering at Cabul, Lahore, or elsewhere. Perhaps it would be easier to imprison him in morocco boards and allow him to be blown with restless violence round about the pendant world, abandoned to critics: whom our lawless and uncertain thoughts imagine howling.